Zilia Sánchez

Heróicas Eróticas en Nueva York

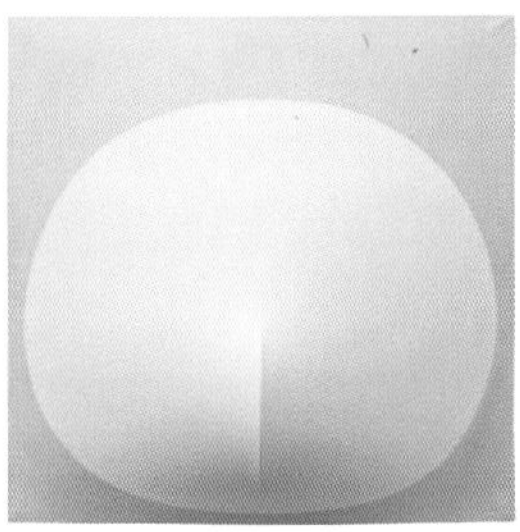

Cover:
Mujer (de la serie el Silencio de Eros), 1965
Woman (of the Silence of Eros series)

Contents

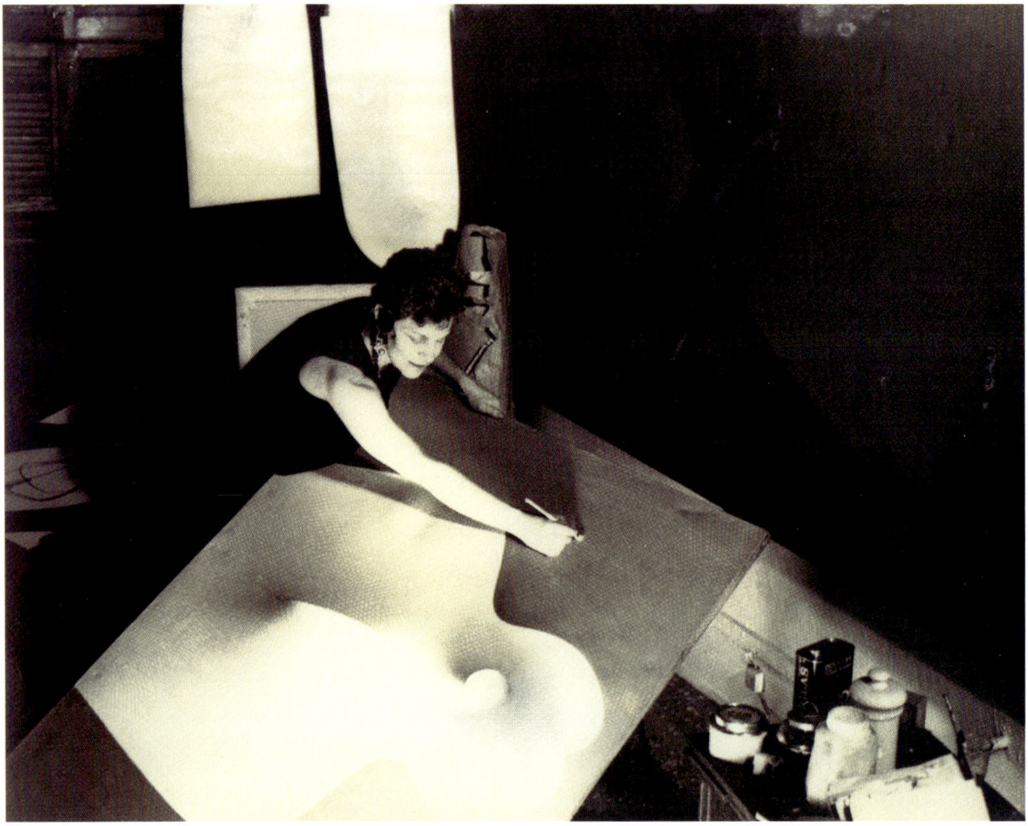

Sánchez working in her studio, 1970

On Zilia Sánchez's Surface

Irene V. Small

"Erotic art makes viewers while pornography makes addicts."
Marta Traba, *"El erotismo y la comunicación"* (1972).

What would it mean to make a "viewer" by means of erotic art? Or rather, what kind of viewer is made by the eroticism of Zilia Sánchez's art? For if Eros, in the classic psychoanalytic framework, is a drive constitutive of the subject–Eros as life, as love, as the instinctual impulse toward creativity and self-realization–it is also a structure of experience, which is to say a sensation embedded in the specificities of aesthetic and bodily encounter. Sánchez's extraordinary shaped canvases tell us as much. Stretched taut over wooden armatures, their membranes painted in neutral tones that pool into nested ovoids, ellipses, clefts, and half-moons, the works oscillate between inciting and reciprocating desire. The desire of the artist who, molding a work's skeleton and then manipulating its tensile skin, treats it as a corpus, an organic entity with formal and emotive energies of its own. And the desire of the viewer, whose motility in relation to the canvas causes its abstracted shapes to expand, contract, slide, dilate, and bloom. To become a "viewer" of Sánchez's work, in short, is to become a subject that emerges with and alongside the work of art.

For the Argentine critic Marta Traba, writing in 1972 in the pages of the vanguard Puerto Rican literary journal *Zona. Carga y Descarga* (which Sánchez herself designed), the eroticism experienced by such a subject was not only aesthetic, but political in import. "Pornography is to eroticism as 'kitsch' is to art," she wrote: the former a consequence of Western capitalism, the latter a means of reinaugurating art's fundamental link to the real.[1] In reestablishing art's affective charge, Traba argued, Sánchez's eroticism offered the viewer an alternative to both the alienation of North American mass culture and the hermetic self-referentiality of its high art. Traba had in mind the hard-edged forms of Minimalism, as did the Paris-based Cuban poet and essayist Severo Sarduy, who for the occasion of Sánchez's exhibition of shaped canvases at the Museo de Historia, Arqueología y Arte de la Universidad de Puerto Rico in 1970, contrasted their allusive, pliable surfaces with the object-like structures of John McCracken, Robert Morris, Sol LeWitt, and

Donald Judd.[2] In aiming for wholly abstract conceptual models, Sarduy claimed, such artists renounced the liquidity, volatility, and voluptuousness of the body. The American critic and curator Lucy Lippard stated as much when she described her 1966 exhibition *Eccentric Abstraction* as departing from the inert facticity of the so-called "structural" sculpture. In contrast to Minimalism's "funerary" impulse, Lippard suggested that the labial, sagging, tumescent, and undulating forms of the new organic work expressed "a wholly sensuous, life-giving element."[3]

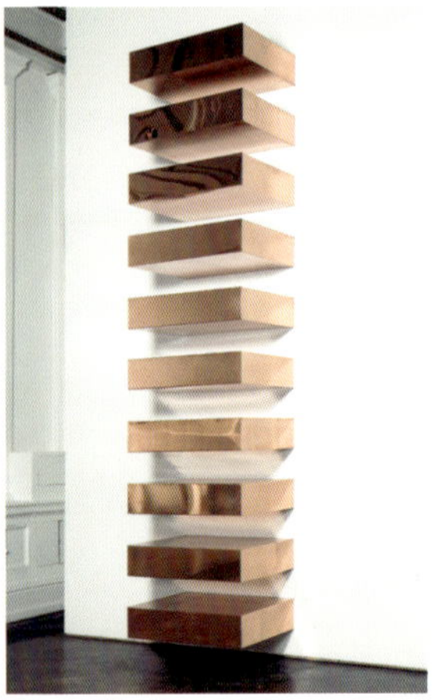

Hindsight reveals that such polarities are schematic at best. The way in which the reflective veneer of a Judd stack sculpture returns the viewer as an image of concatenated fragments annuls the fiction of a bodiless abstraction. Eva Hesse's latex and resin modules likewise demonstrate that repetition is at once mechanical and serial, excessive and fleshy.[4] Eros and Thanatos are necessarily intertwined.

And yet the erotic quality Sarduy and Traba first observed in Sánchez's work remains as elusive as it is unusual. Not simply because the Cuban-born Sánchez, who from the late 1950s to the early 1970s traveled between Havana, Madrid, and New York before settling in San Juan, enacted an artistic and geopolitical nomadism that circumvents a univocal tethering of style to place. But perhaps more urgently because Sánchez's works appear to transform an erotic paradigm premised on metaphoric interiority into one organized as literal *exteriority*, that is, into a poetics of surface itself. In the paradigm of interiority, the canvas, figured as female body, remains entrenched within a hetero-normative interpretive regime (witness the "penetration" of the support in Lucio Fontana's slashed *Concetti Spaziali (Spatial Concepts)*, or the vaginal tropes that crowd Lee Bontecou's velvet-lined

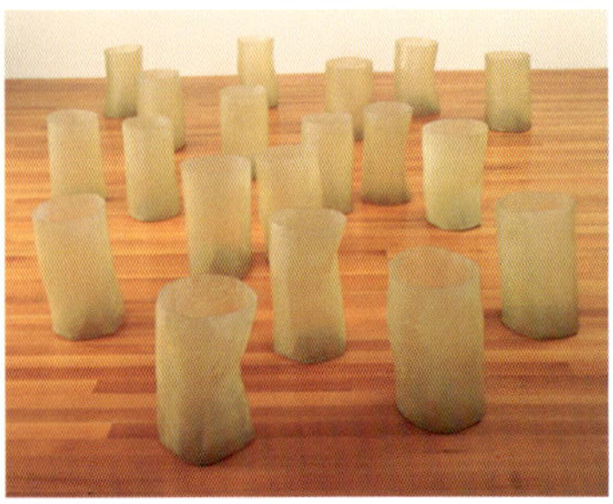

Donald Judd. *Untitled*, 1969
Eva Hesse. *Repetition Nineteen III*, 1968

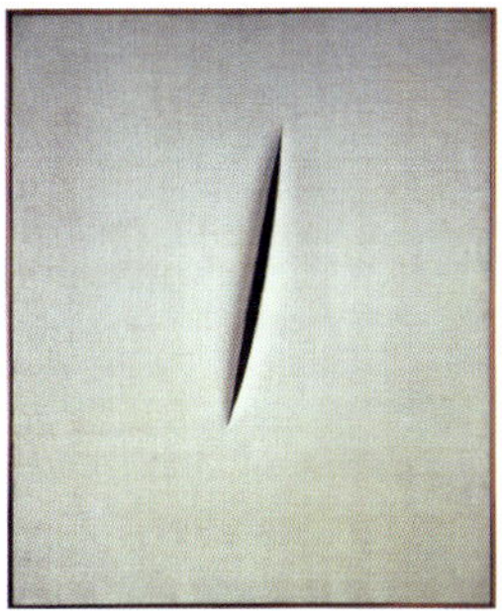

voids). By contrast, Sánchez's treatment of her canvases as extensive surface—"erotic topologies," as she terms them—constitutes a queering of the work's associative content, but more importantly, of the means by which this content is apprehended and felt.

Consider, for example, a suite of drawings from the late 1960s titled *El Significado del Significante (The Signified of the Signifier)*, made in the same years that Sánchez began to construct her shaped, modular works. In the drawings, stippled dots cluster and radiate in order to delineate bulbous sacs and delicate tentacles. These forms attenuate and dissolve against the blank surface of the support, radically destabilizing the relationship between figure and ground. Here the semblance of a breast is demarcated out of negative space; to its side, an aggregation of similar mounds are formed through the suggestion of contour; just below, a nipple-like or clitoral protrusion gathers tactility from a density of marks; this same shape, now repeated and distributed as an isolated motif, becomes flat and abstract. Another drawing likewise performs absence, accumulation, and supplementarity in the same breath: just as the viewer projects a doubled roundness onto an implied buttock or breast, the imagined part materializes as a self-enclosed form dislocated in space. Reference and association—but also tension and dispersal—thus build laterally, through an allusive spreading or unfurling in which marked and unmarked share equally in a given drawing's pictorial and affective force. Signifiers do not secure signifieds but rather displace them as the eye moves across the page. It is precisely by means of this oblique sideways movement, moreover, that eroticism is fueled or held at bay.

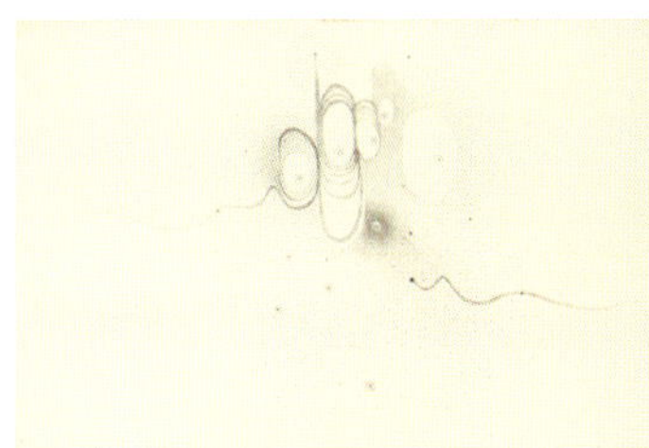

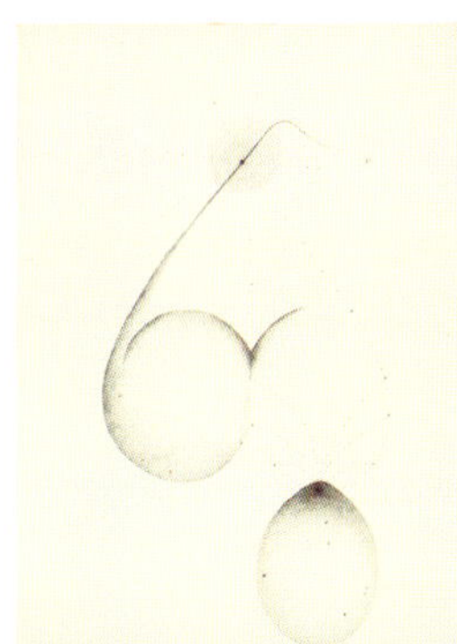

Lucio Fontana. *Concetto Spaziale Attesa [Waiting]*, 1960
Zilia Sánchez. *El Significado del Significante*, 1968 | pp. 52 - 53
Zilia Sánchez. *El Significado del Significante*, 1968 | p. 57

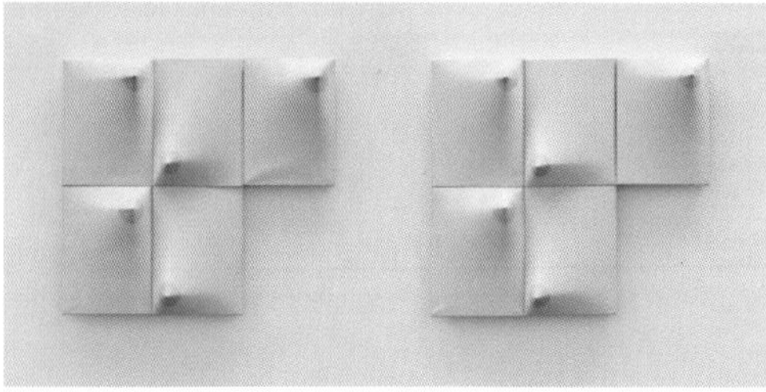

In Sánchez's shaped canvases, this gliding displacement is intensified in the form of topologies literalized in space. In her *Módulos Infinitos* (*Infinite Modules)* and *Troyanas, Polípticos* (*Trojans*, *Polyptychs*), arranged in odd numbers to resist the closure and symmetry of the grid, for example, sequential panels distribute visual foci across a field, which in turn coalesce as tactile pattern or pulsating rhythm when seen from the front or side. Twinned panels in which protruding discs and curved mounts generate symbiotic pairs, meanwhile, are reactivated by ambient light, which allow the panels to redraw—even caress—the contours of neighboring planes by means of cast shadows.[5] Even in single canvases such as *Mujer (de la serie el Silencio de Eros)* (*Woman (of the Silence of Eros series)*) in which a projecting ridge elongates a circle into an oval, or *Sin título* (*Untitled)*, in which an oblong crescent destabilizes the swelling movement of its enclosed semisphere, the intimate, and specifically female, cartography of Sánchez's work stems from surface intensities that are differential rather than dichotomous in effect.

It is in relation to this differential aspect of surface, too, that we can begin to understand Sánchez's temporality, which often resists the linearity of strict chronology as well as the finitude of individual works. As Sarduy already noted in 1970, the "successive transformations" of Sánchez's modules, titles, and motifs "refuse the notion of origins... None of these canvases," he wrote, "is the 'first,' 'original' or 'true'".[6] Indeed, Sánchez sometimes shifts the orientation of her panels, partners them with "sisters," returns to "tattoo" them with drawings, sometimes over a space of years.

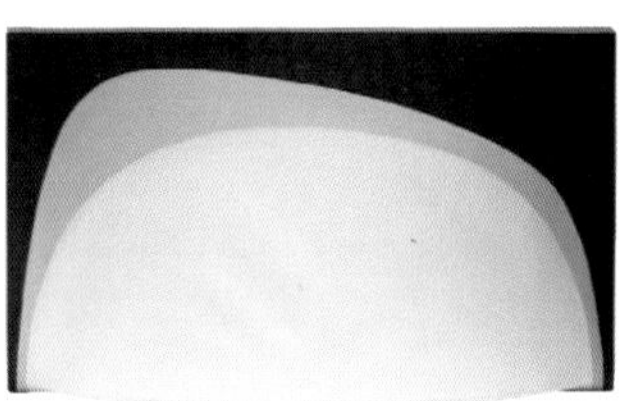

Zilia Sánchez. *Troyanas, políptico,* 1999 | pp. 40 - 41
Zilia Sánchez. *Mujer (de la serie el Silencio de Eros),* 1965 | p. 13
Zilia Sánchez. *Sin título,* 1990 | p. 43

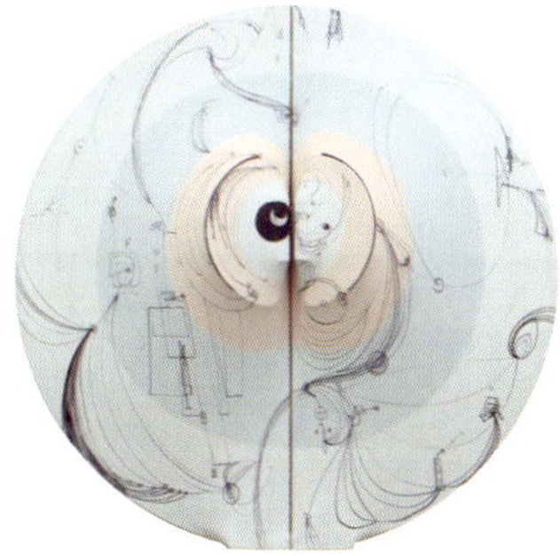

In a work such as *Lunar con Tatuaje (Moon with Tattoo)*, for instance, begun in the late 1960s but only finished in the mid-1990s, linear inscriptions traced across the work's painted surface index a velocity distinct from the slow duration of its neutral chromatic bands. Mapped one upon the other, drawing and painting stretch and collapse time, as if to register the varying modalities of our gaze. Of course erotic time, too, is neither linear nor sequential, but circles back to its locus of desire, pressurizing, reprising, defamiliarizing anew. To apprehend the work of art as an erotic entity is therefore to acknowledge the unpredictable organicism, achronicity, and contingency that erupt when a material object is approached as a dynamic, reciprocal field.

To reiterate the question: what kind of viewer is made by the eroticism of Sánchez's art? As her poetics of surface makes clear, Sánchez's work does not invite interpretation or entry, as if to locate a static content, identity, or body "behind" the work of art. Such a hermeneutics would imply a corresponding fixity on the part of the viewer. Rather, Sánchez's topologies solicit a subject in process: a subject formed and continually reformed in the lateral slippage between self and work.

Irene V. Small is Assistant Professor of Art and Archaeology at Princeton University, where she teaches modern and contemporary art with a transnational focus. She is an affiliated faculty member of the Program in Latin American Studies and the Program in Media and Modernity. Her book *Hélio Oiticica: Folding the Frame* is forthcoming from University of Chicago Press in 2015.

1. Marta Traba, "El erotismo y la comunicación," *Zona de Carga y Descarga*, San Juan, Puerto Rico (November - December 1972): 11.
2. Severo Sarduy, "Las `Topologías Eróticas' de Zilia Sánchez," in *Zilia Sánchez: Estructuras en Secuencia* (San Juan: Museo de la Universidad de Puerto Rico, 1970).
3. Lucy Lippard, "Eccentric Abstraction," *Art International* 10, no. 9 (November 1966): 28.
4. On the imbrication of the industrial and organic drives, see Mignon Nixon, "O+X," *October*, no. 119 (Winter 2007): 6 - 20.
5. For a compelling description of this process and its relation to Sánchez's typographic compositions, see Benigno Trigo, "Zona, Carga y Descarga: Minor Literature in a Penal Colony," *MLN* 124, no. 2 (March 2009): 481 - 508.
6. Sarduy, "Las 'Topologías Eróticas' de Zilia Sanchez."

Zilia Sánchez. *Lunar con Tatuaje*, c. 1968-96 | pp. 18 - 19

Paintings

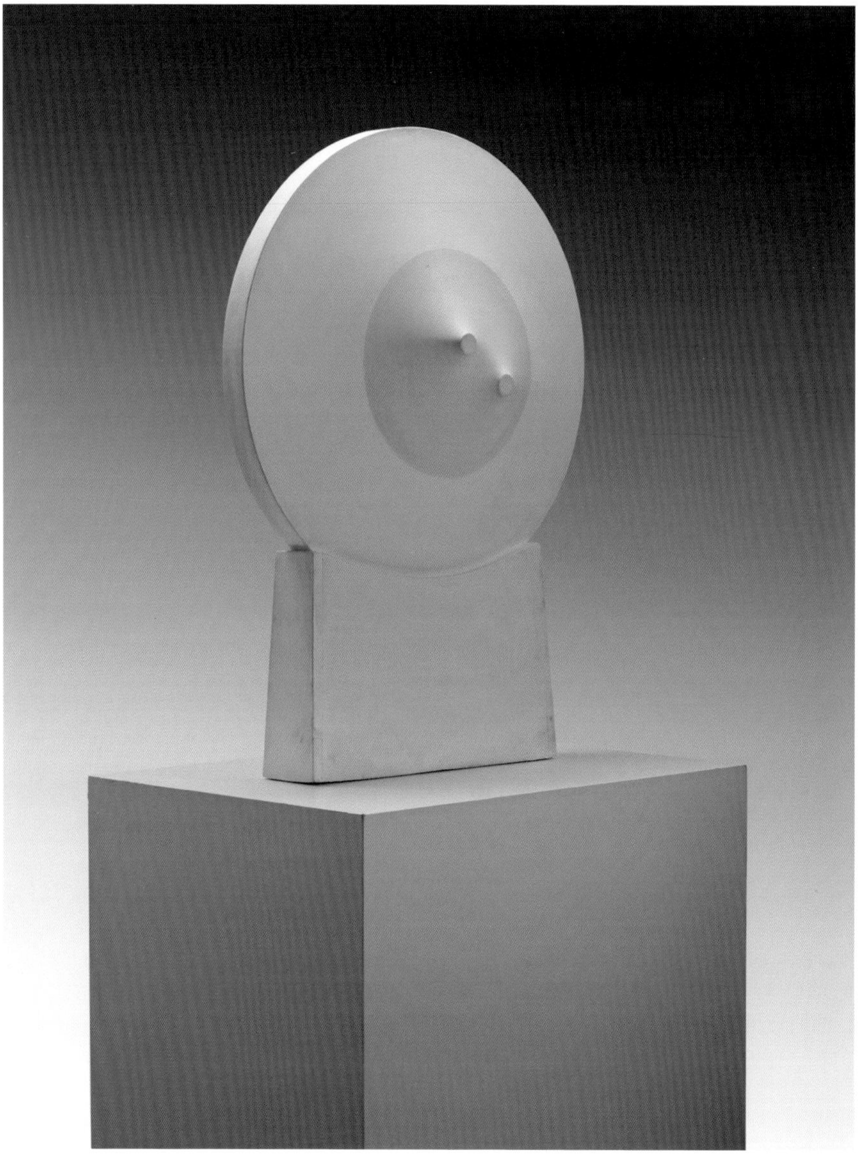

 Lunar blanco, 1964 | White moon

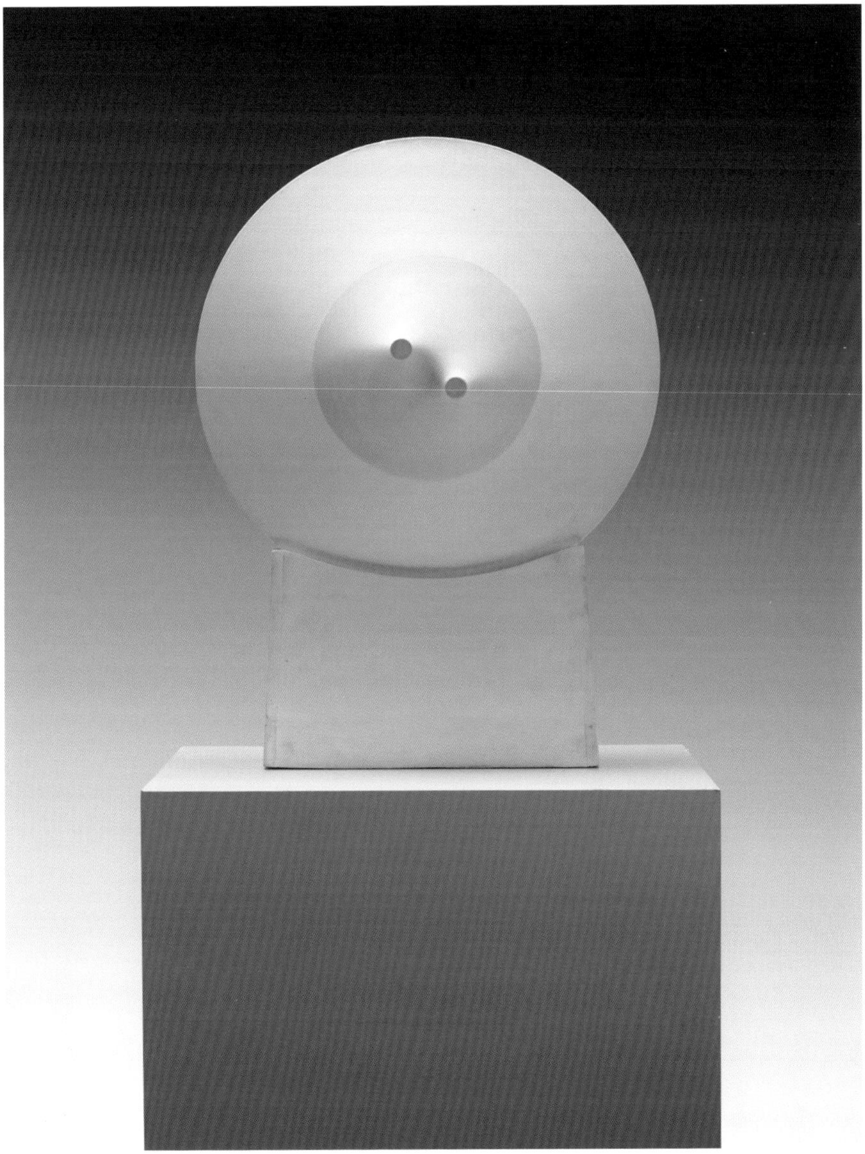

Mujer (de la serie el Silencio de Eros), 1965 | Woman (of the Silence of Eros series)

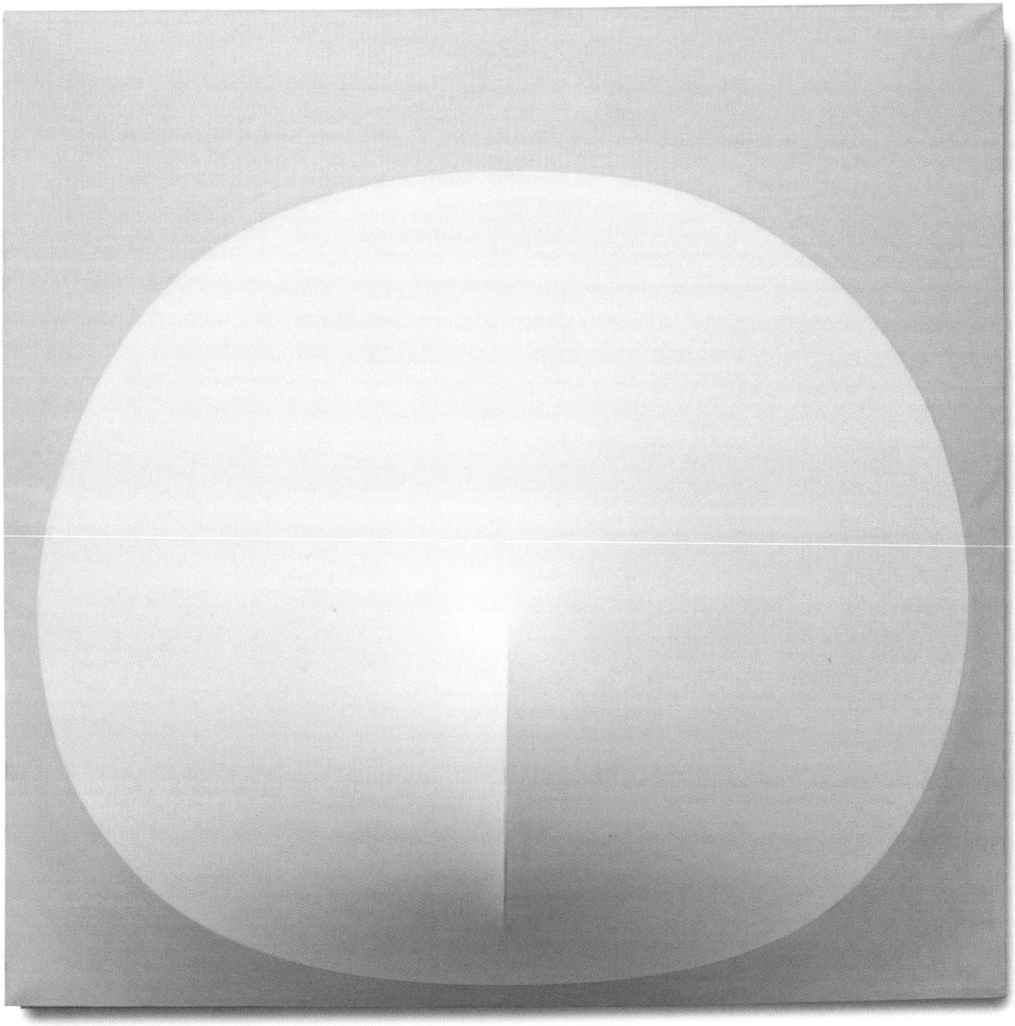

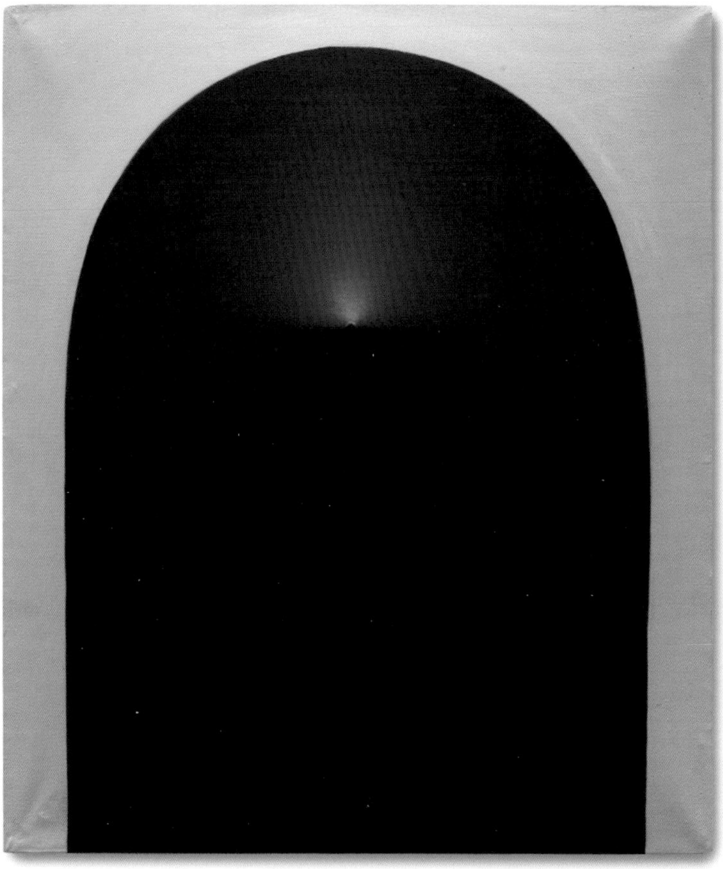

 Amazona, 1968 | Amazon

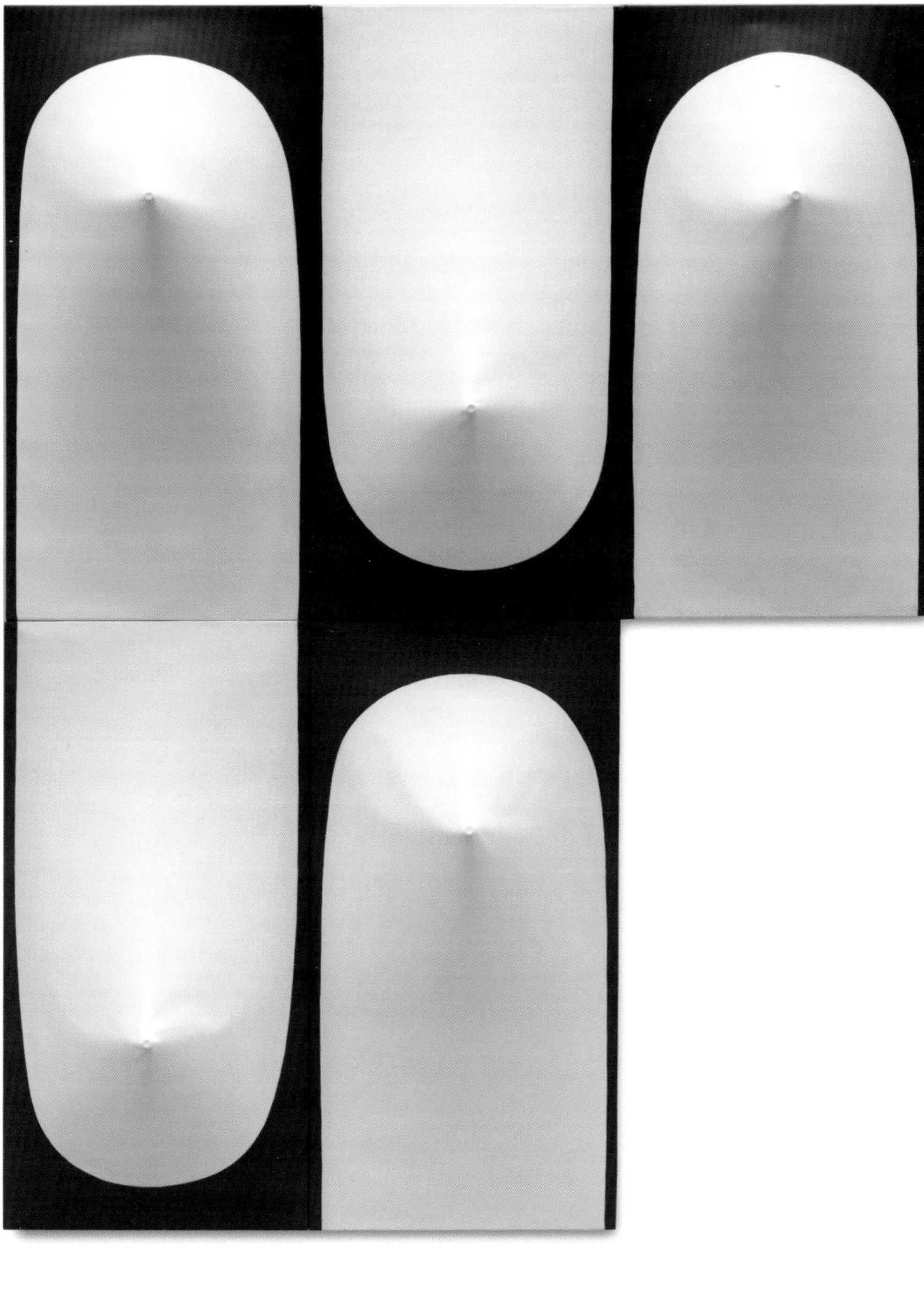

Troyanas, políptico (de la serie Módulos Infinitos), 1967 | Trojans, polyptych (of the Infinite Modules series)

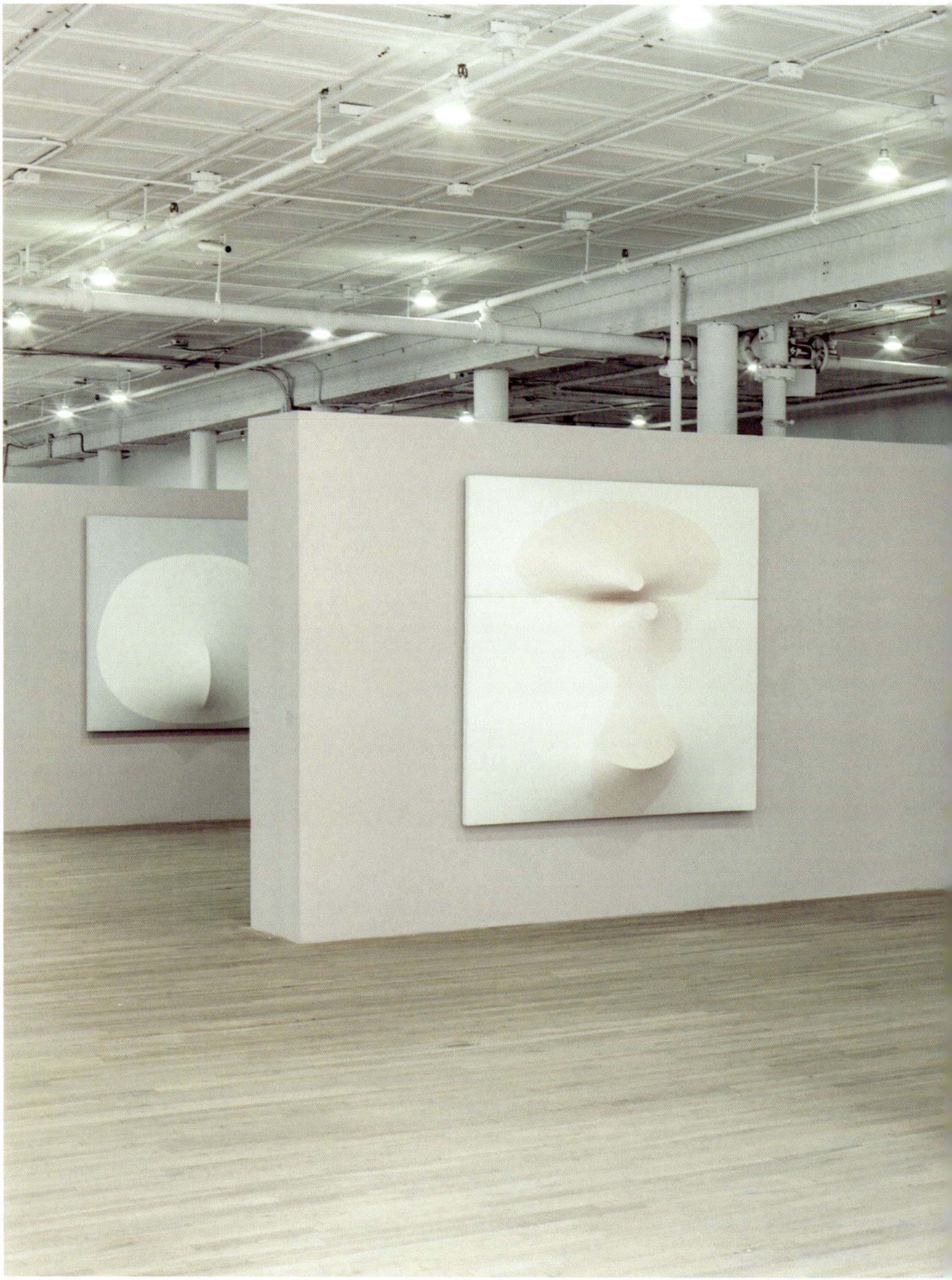

 Installation view: Artists Space, New York, 2013

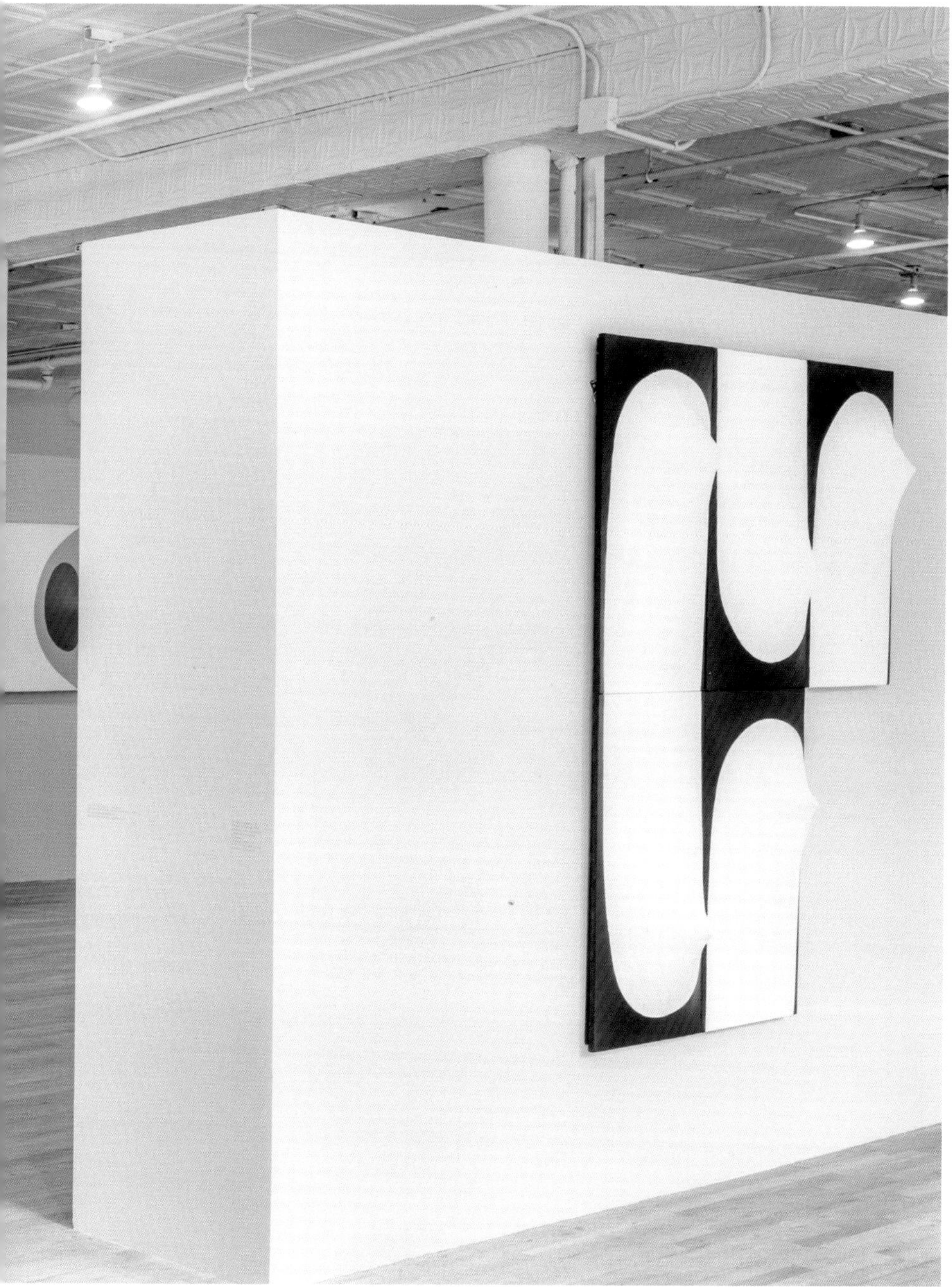

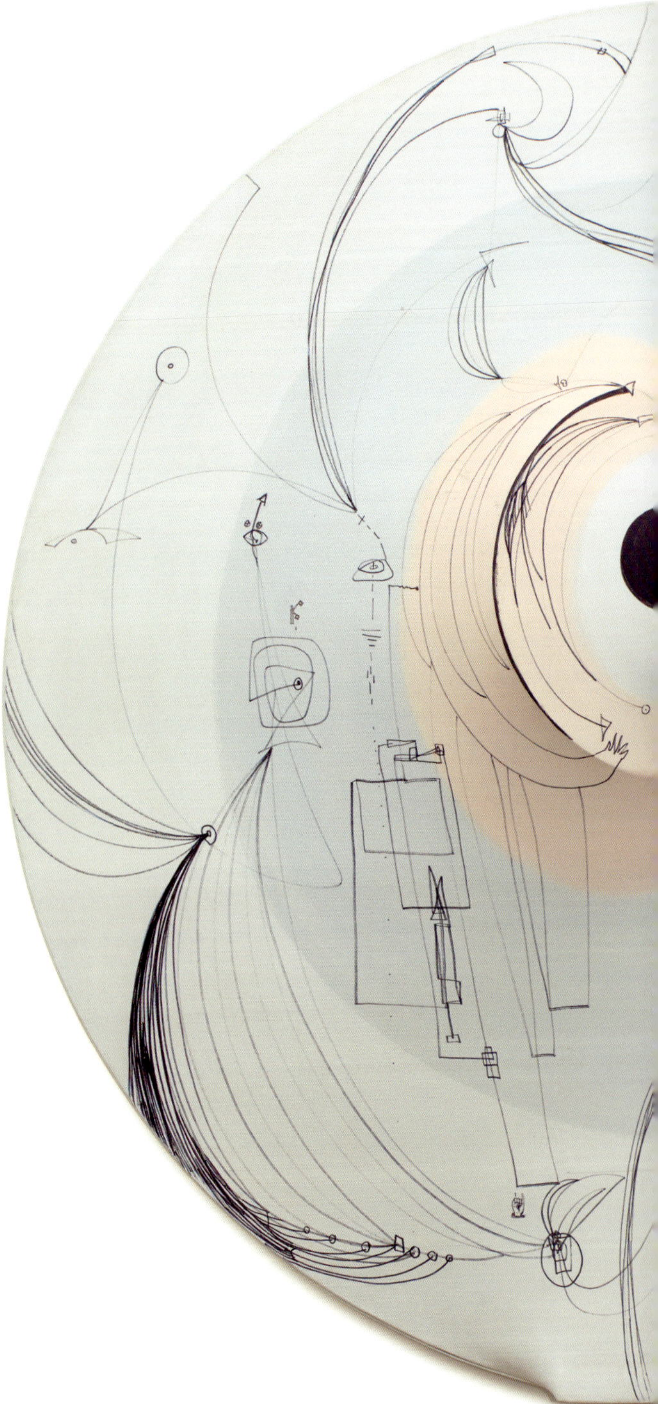

 Lunar con Tatuaje, c. 1968-96 | Moon with Tattoo

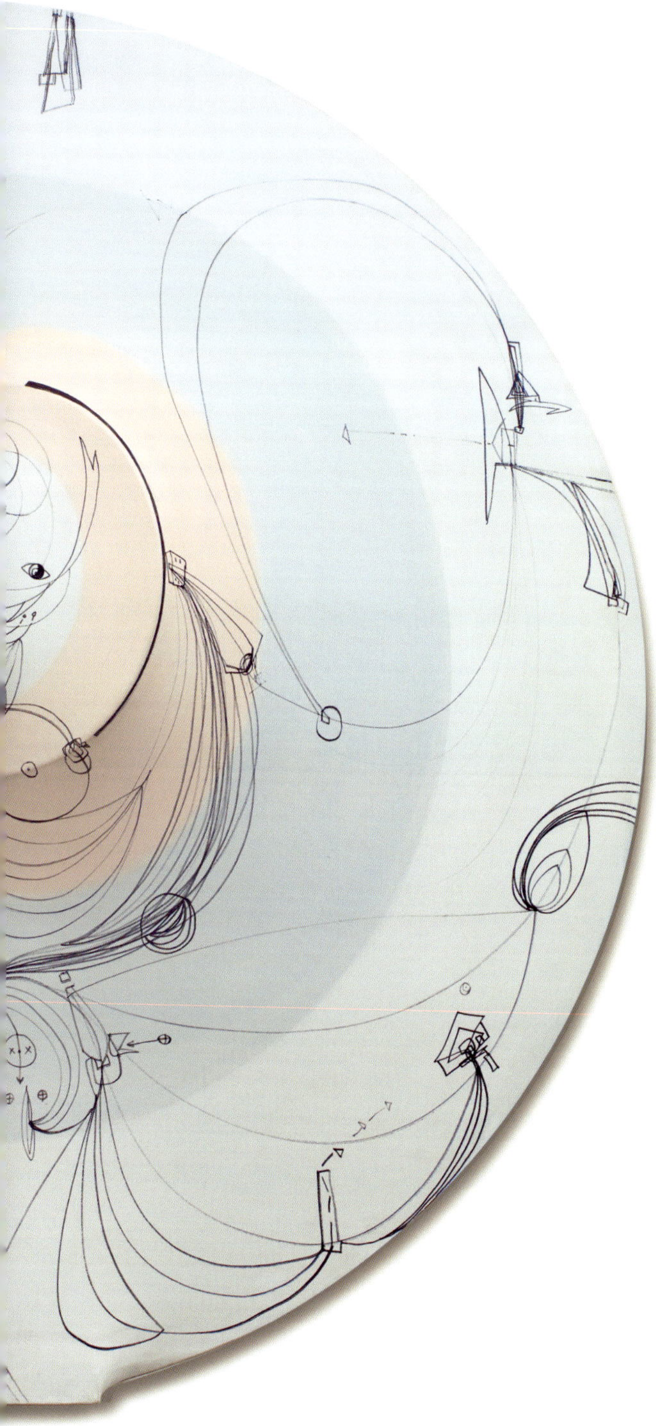

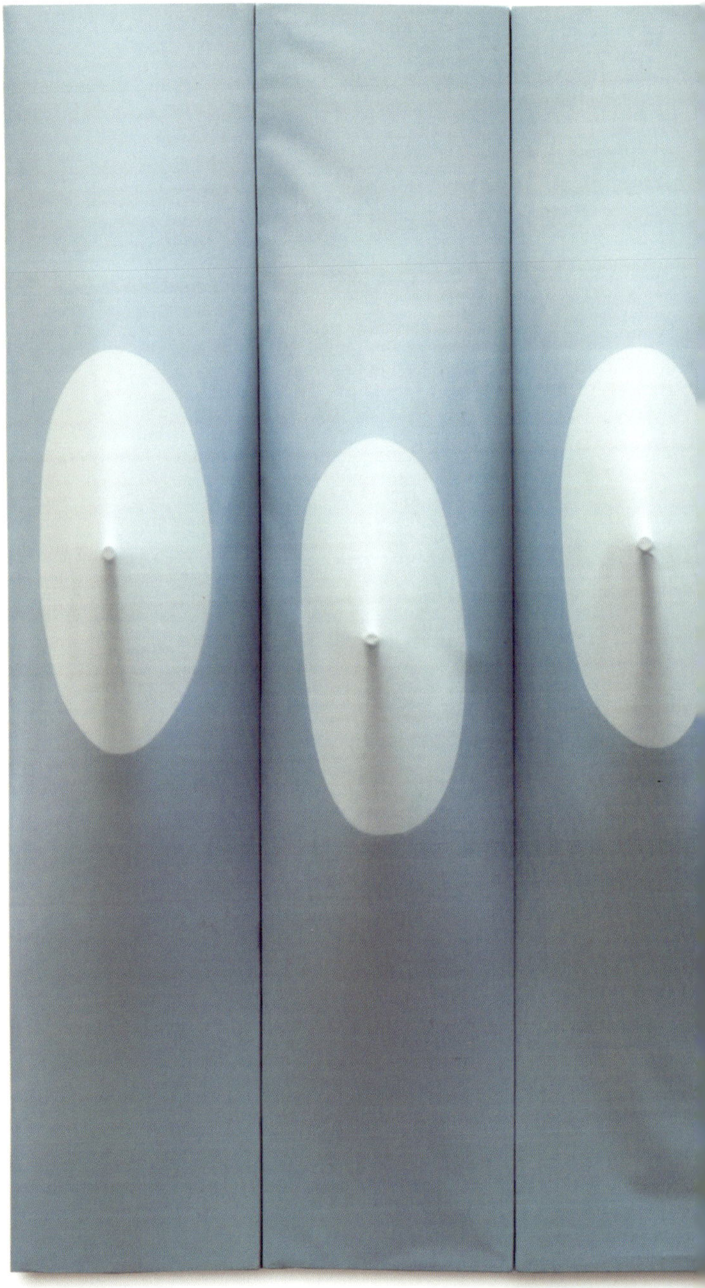

 Amazonas, 1972 | Amazons

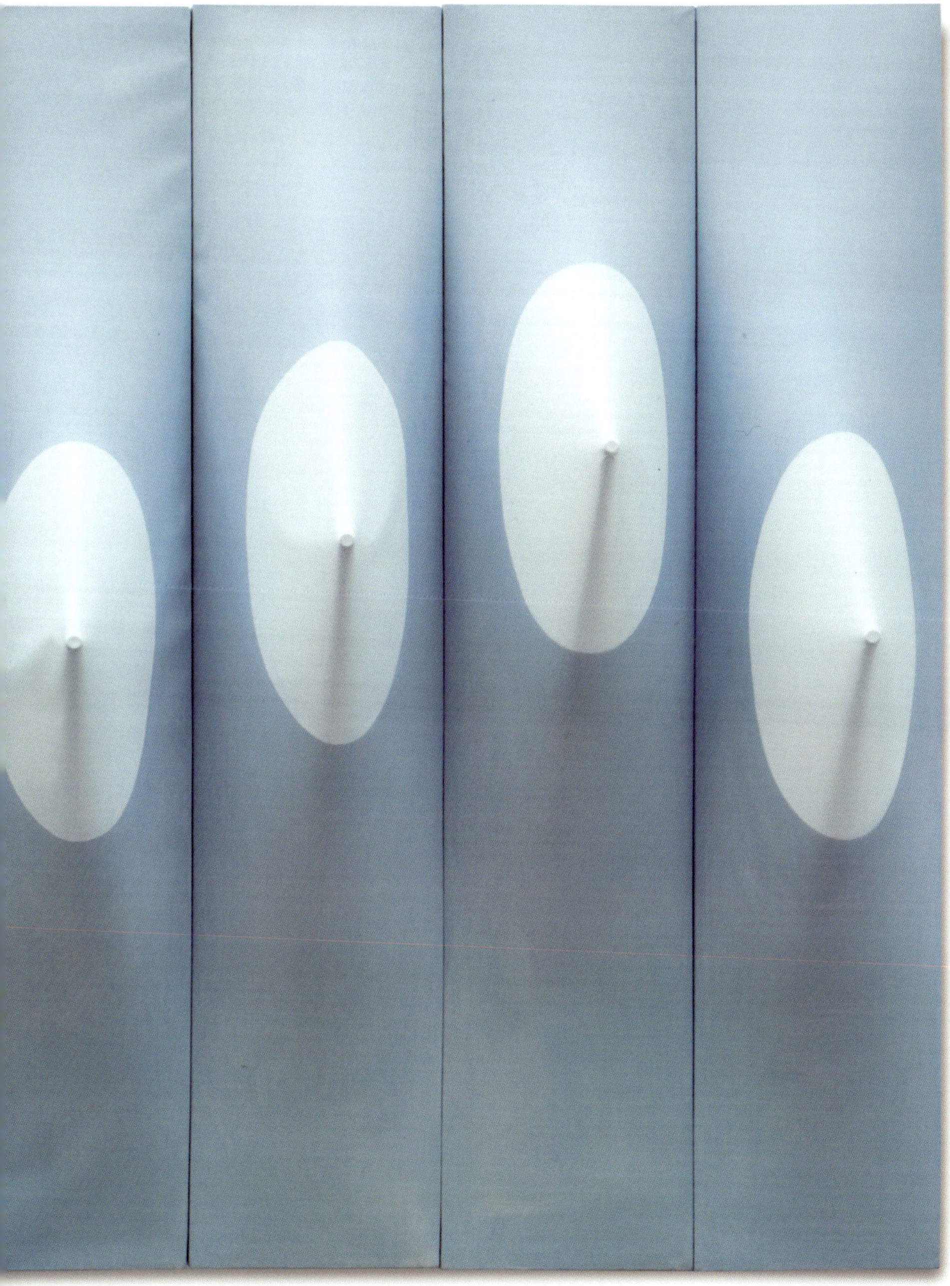

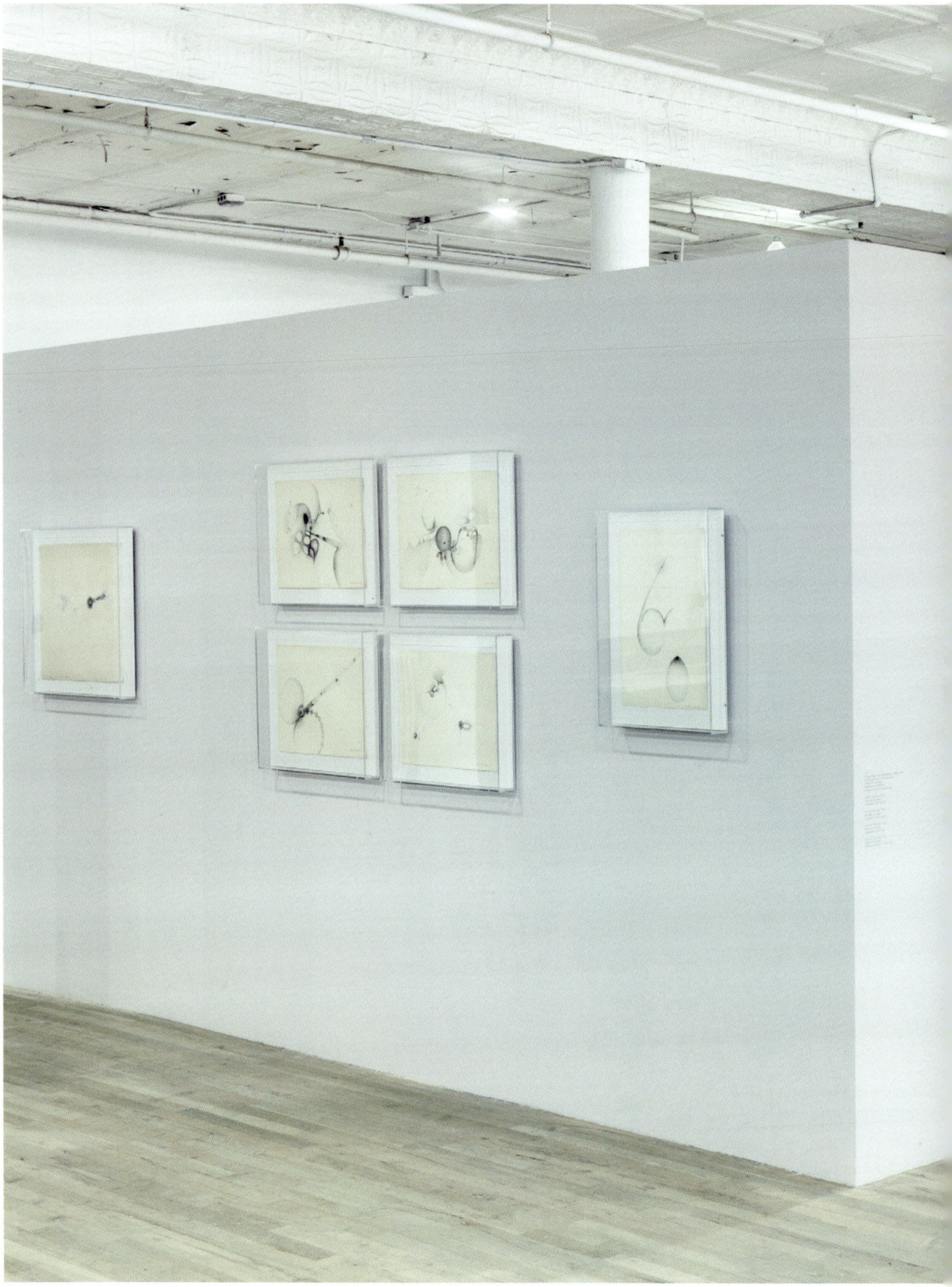

 Installation view: Artists Space, New York, 2013

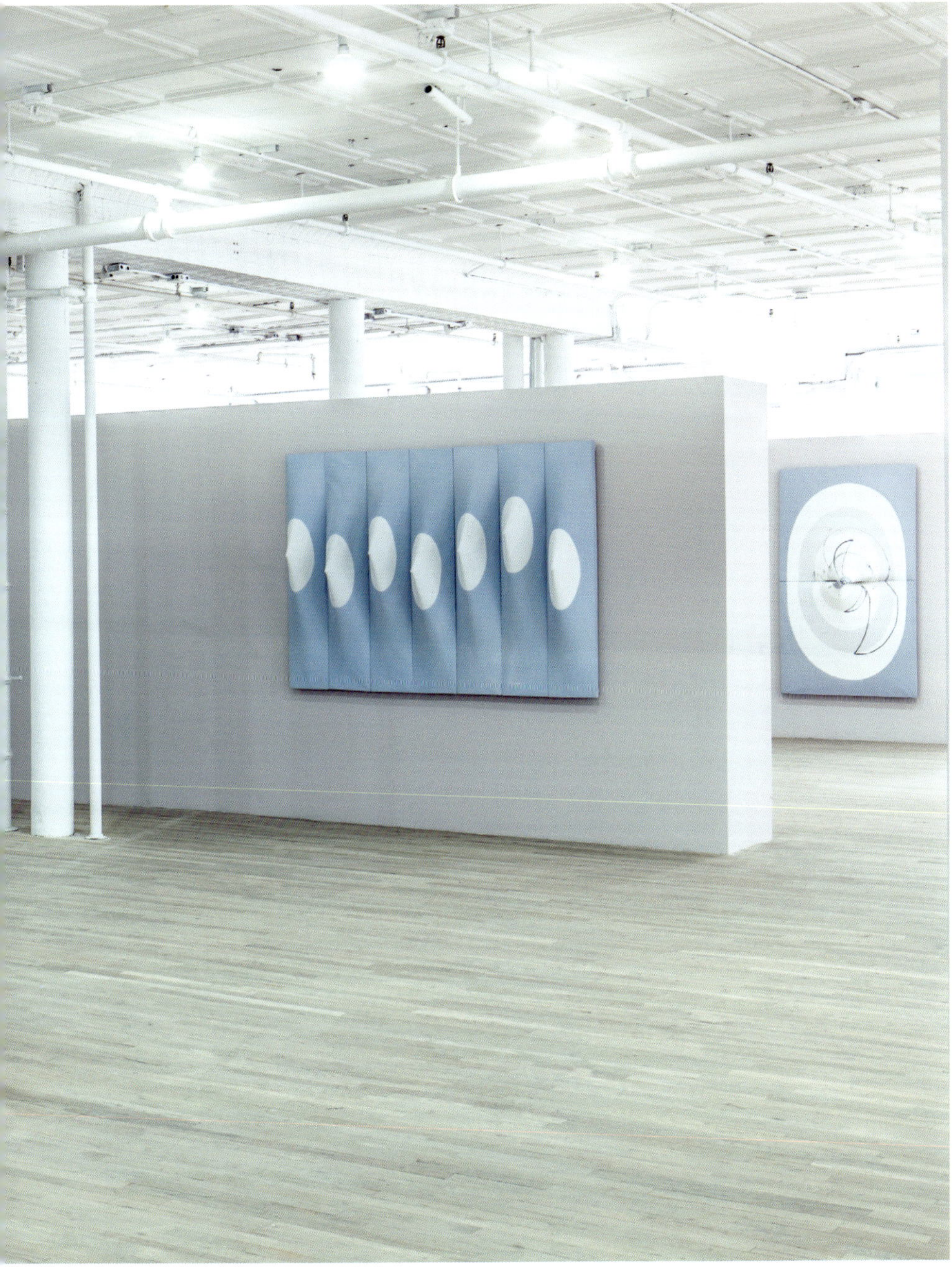

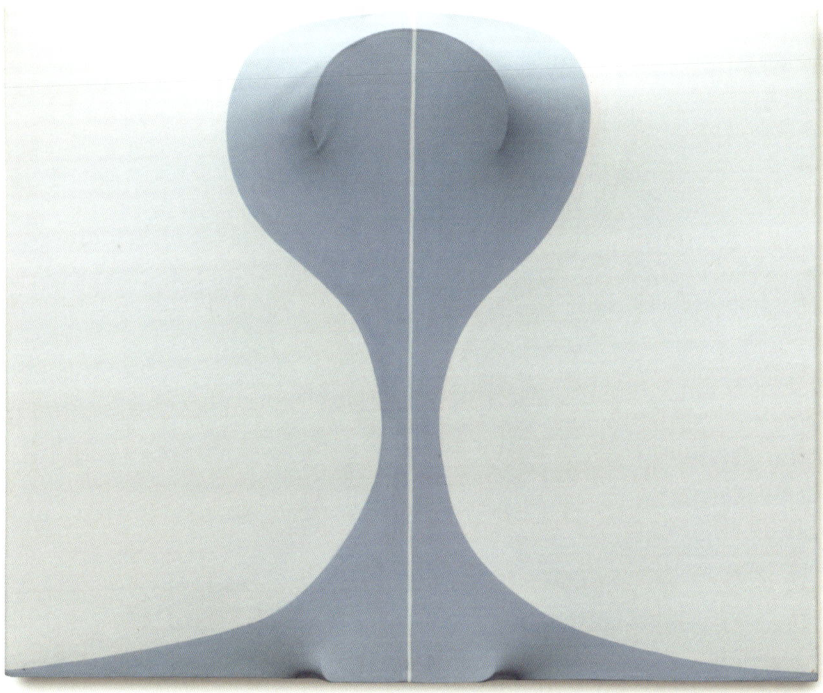

 Antigonía, 1970 | Antigone

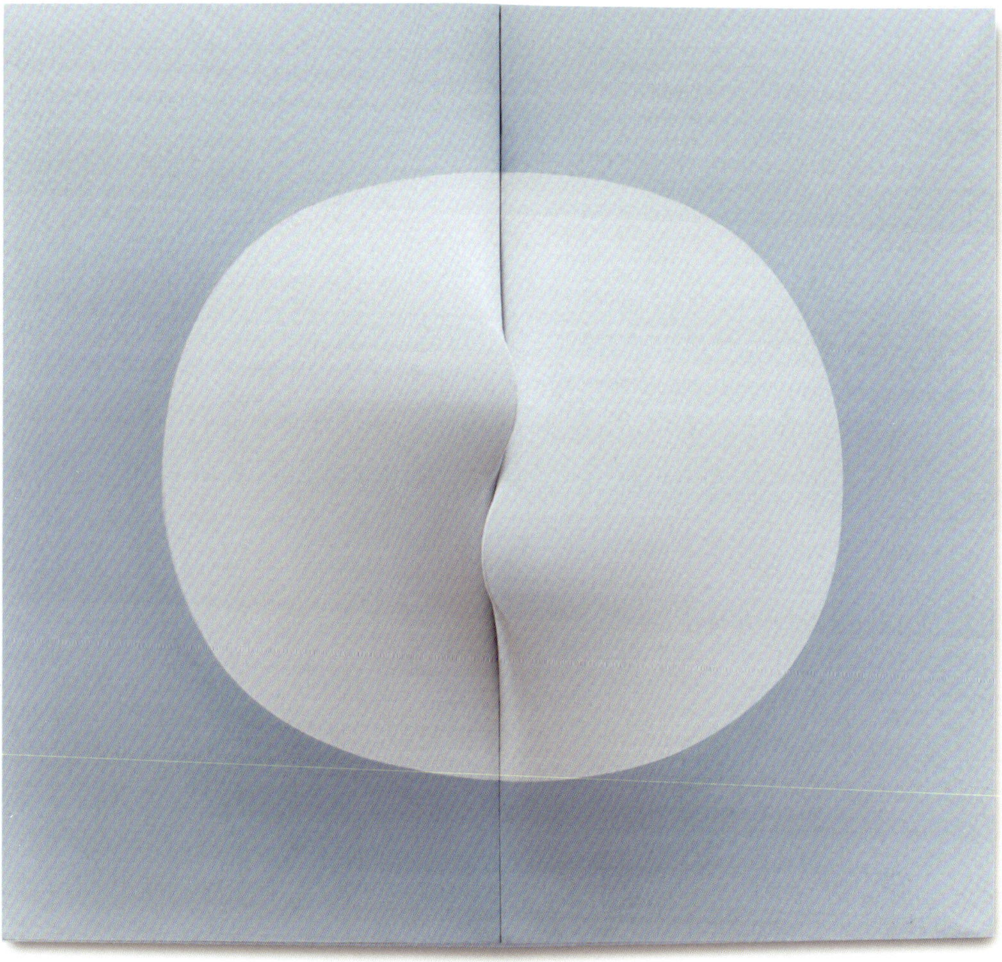

Lunar V, c. 1973 | Moon V

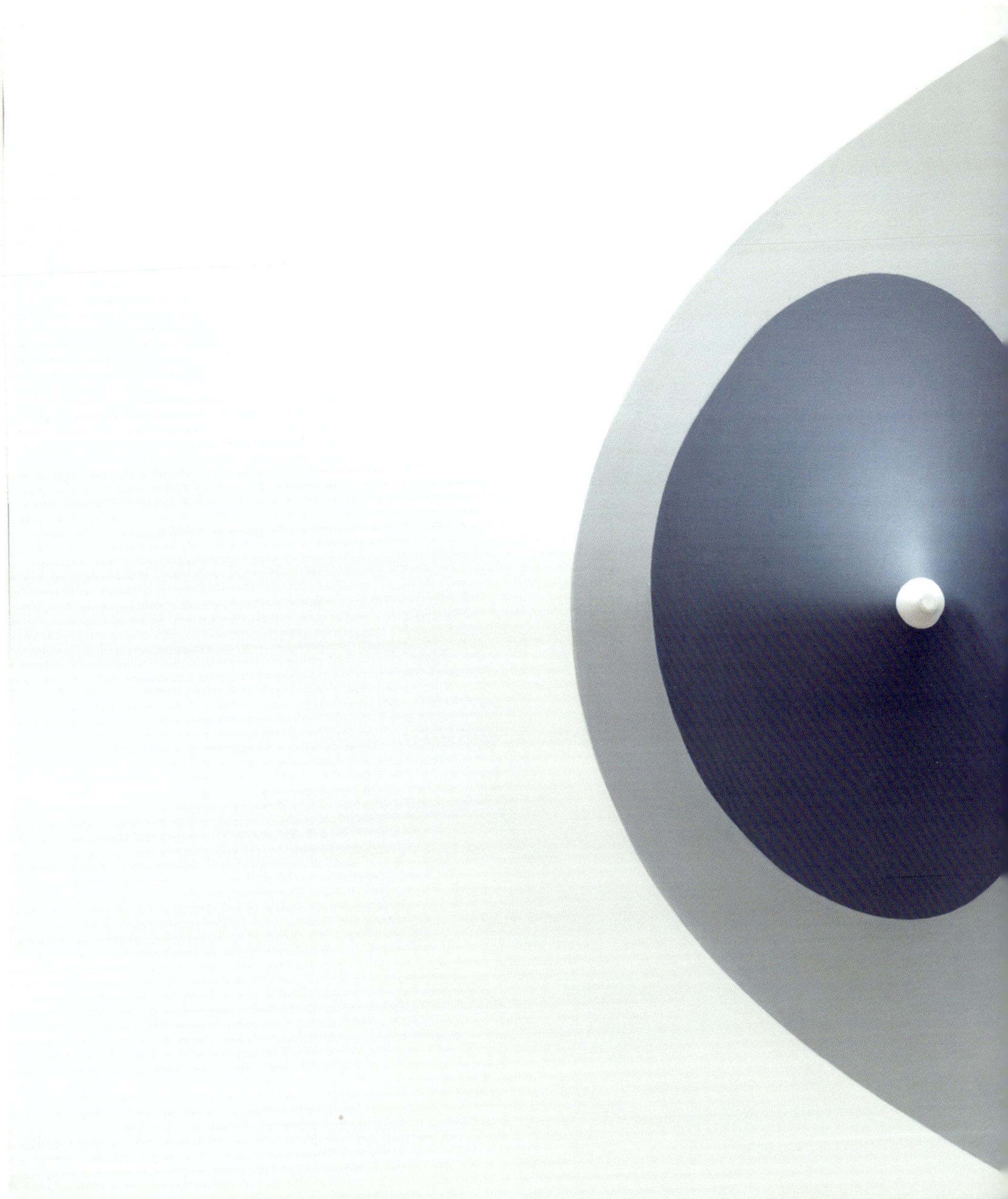

Troyanas, díptico, 1975 | Trojans, diptych

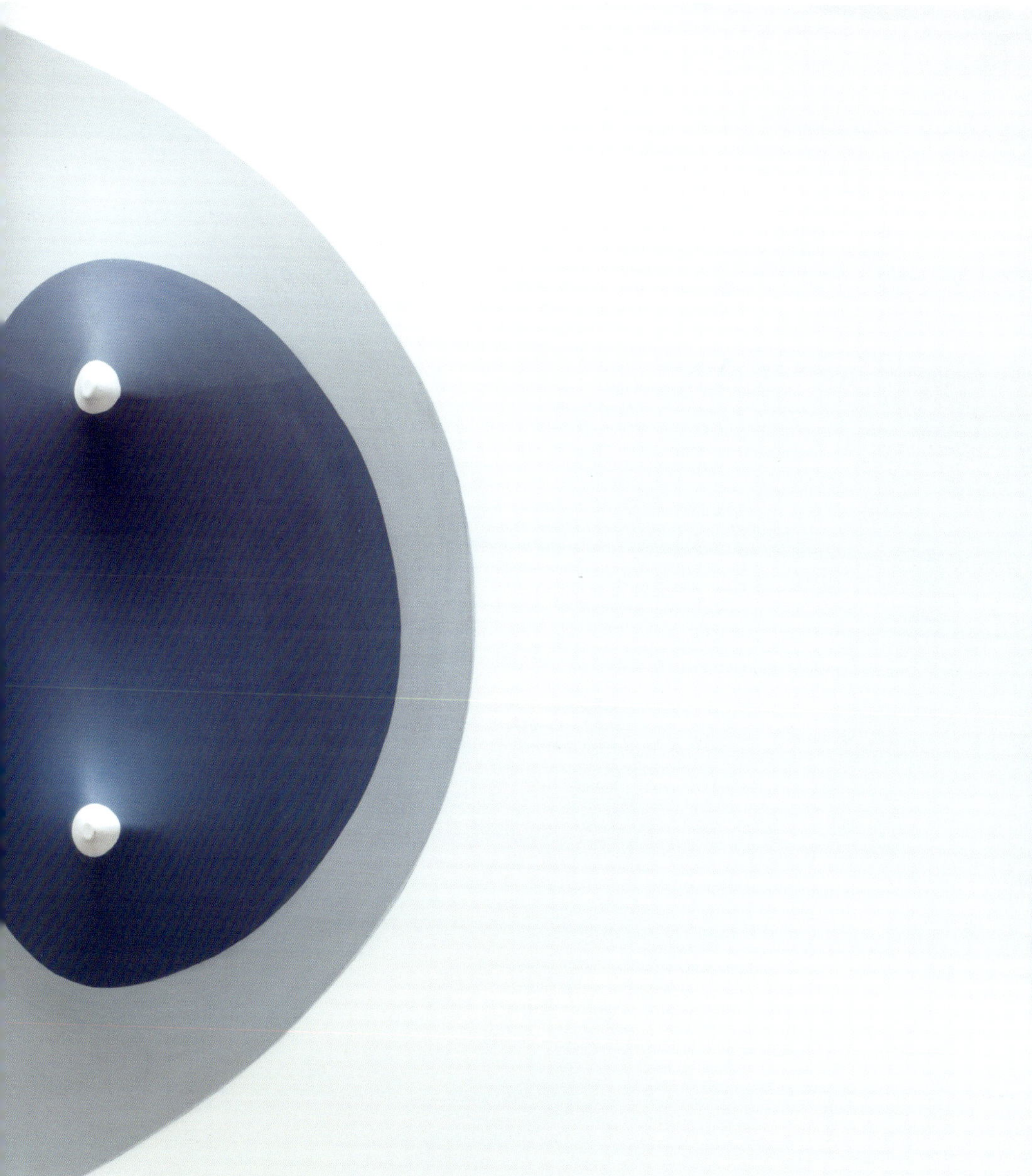

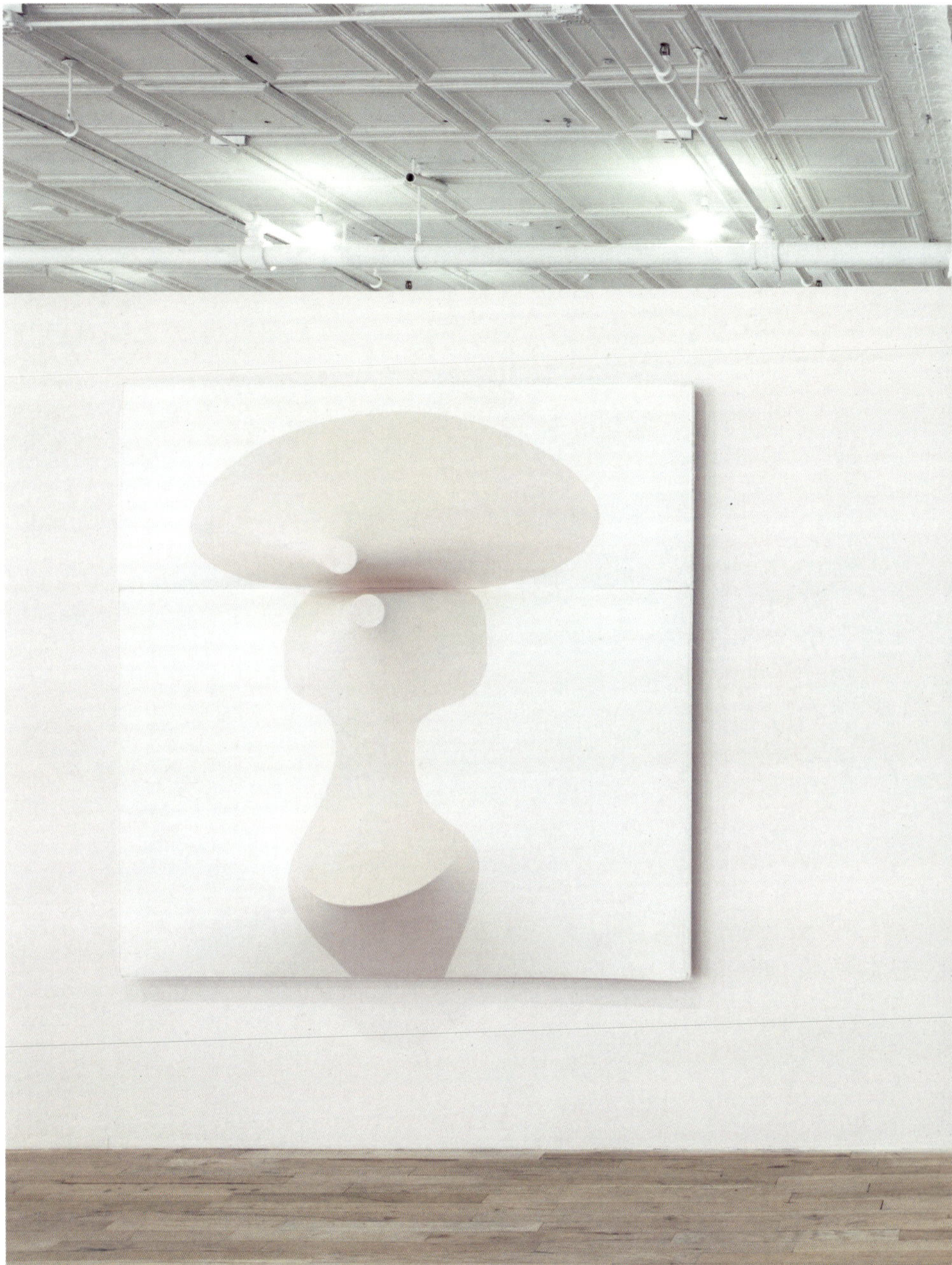

 Installation view: Artists Space, New York, 2013

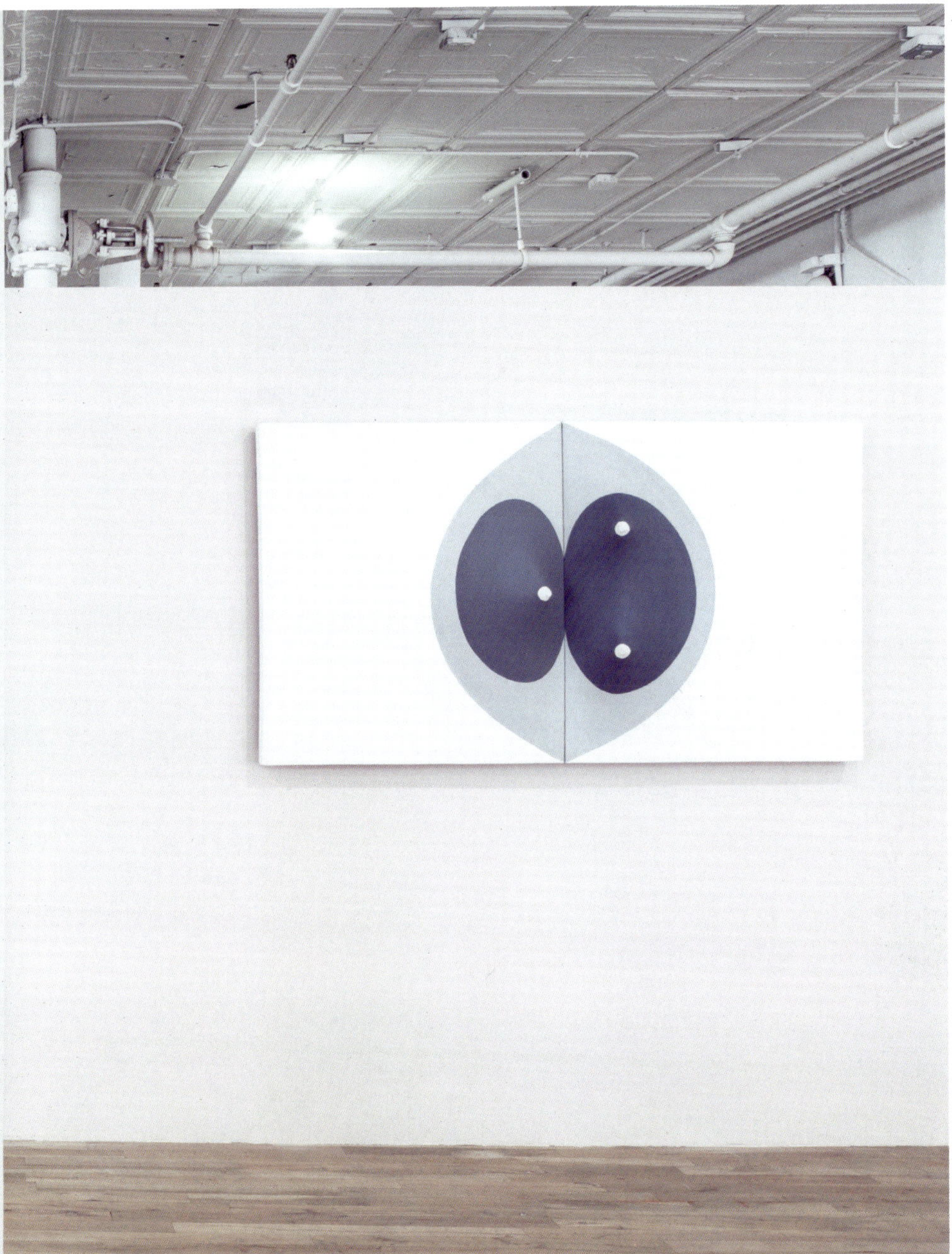

Eros, 1976

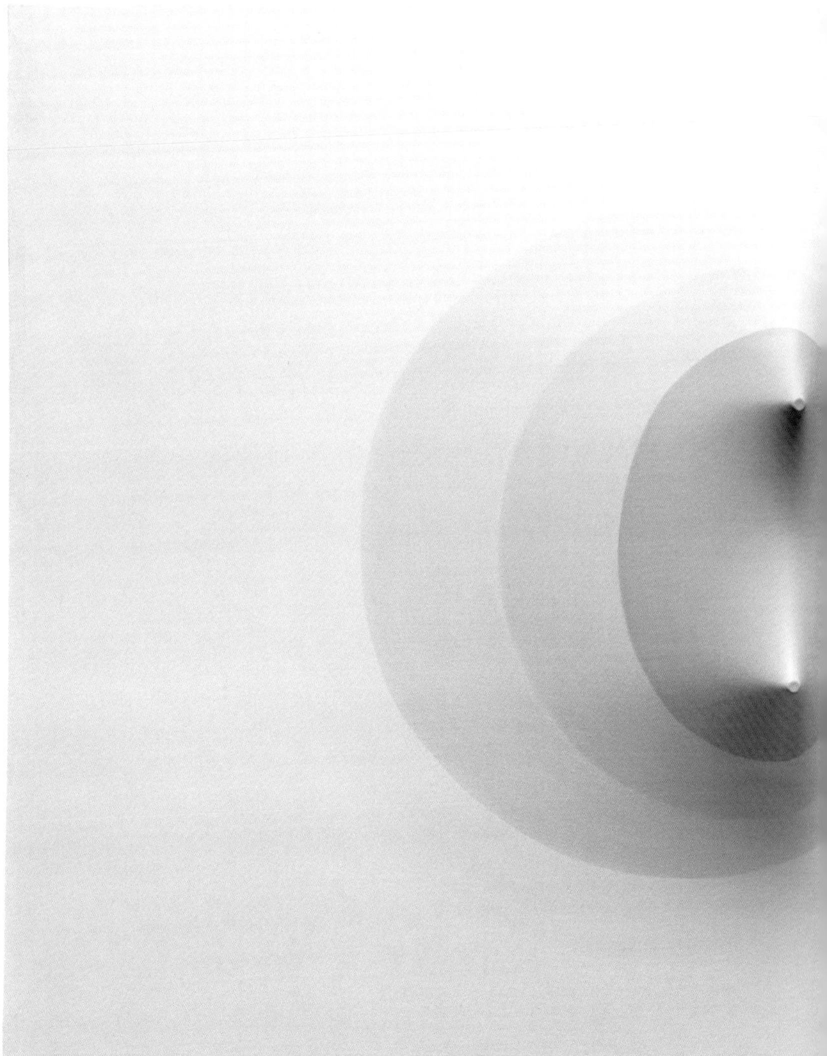

 Amazonas (de la serie Topologías), 1978 | Amazons (of the Topologies series)

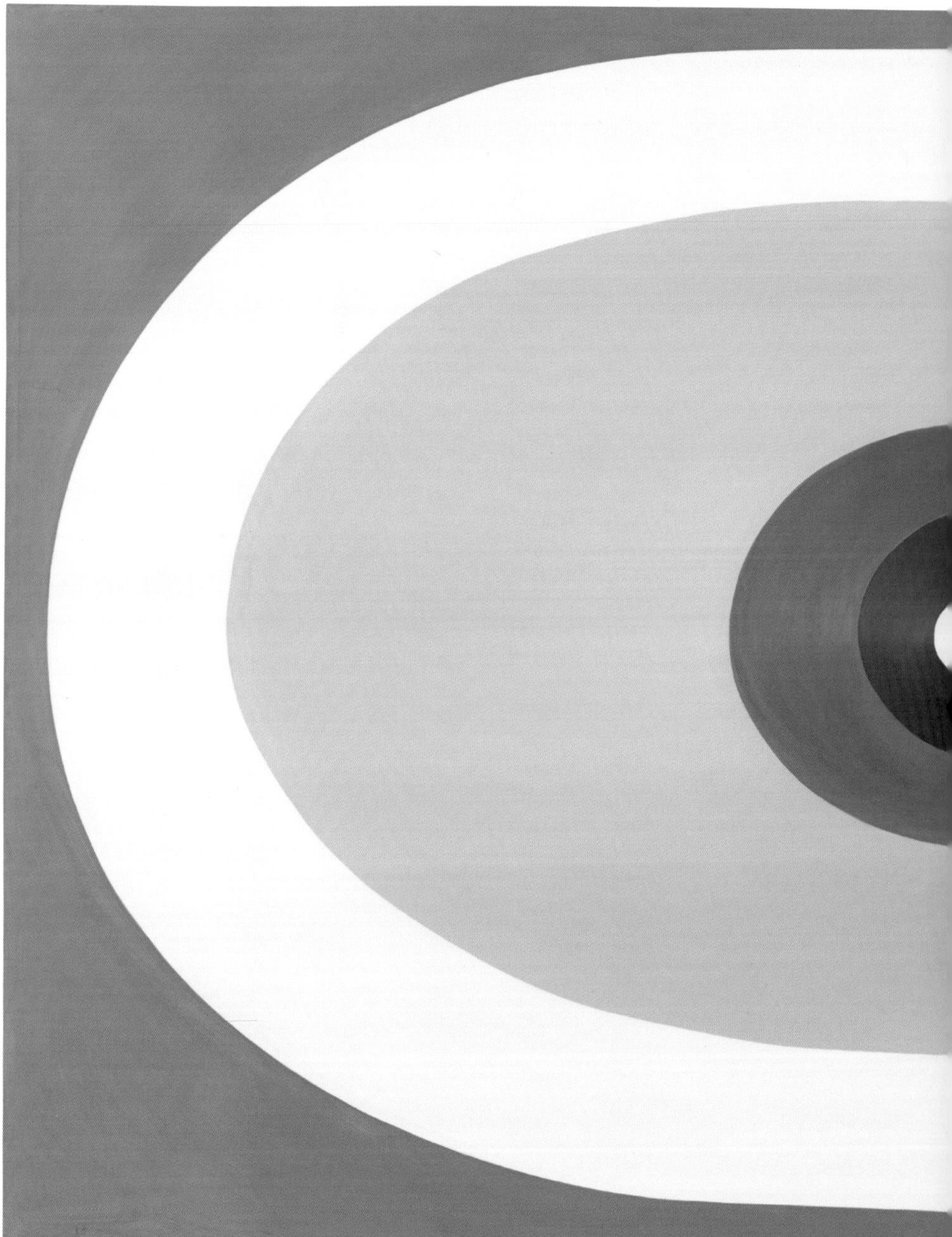

Sin título, 1978 | Untitled

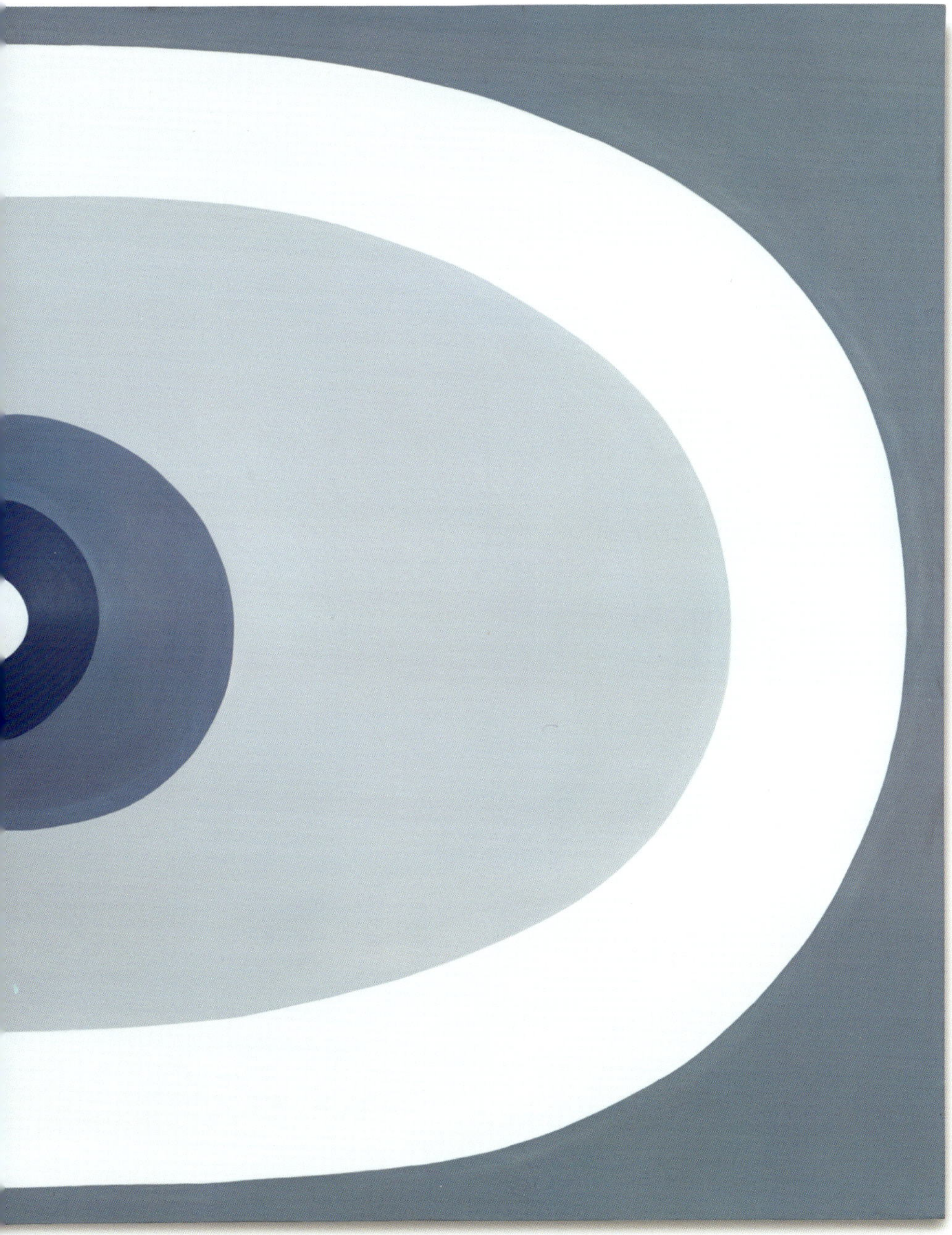

 Módulo infinito, 1978 | Infinite module

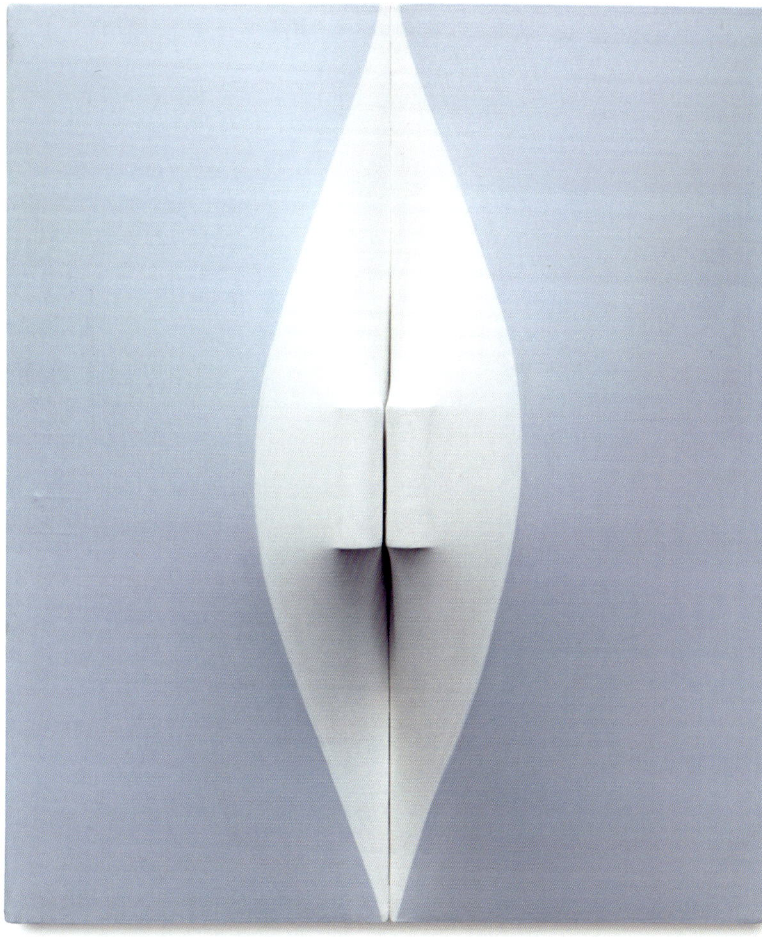

El Silencio de Eros (de la serie Topologías), 1982-90 | The Silence of Eros (of the Topologies series)

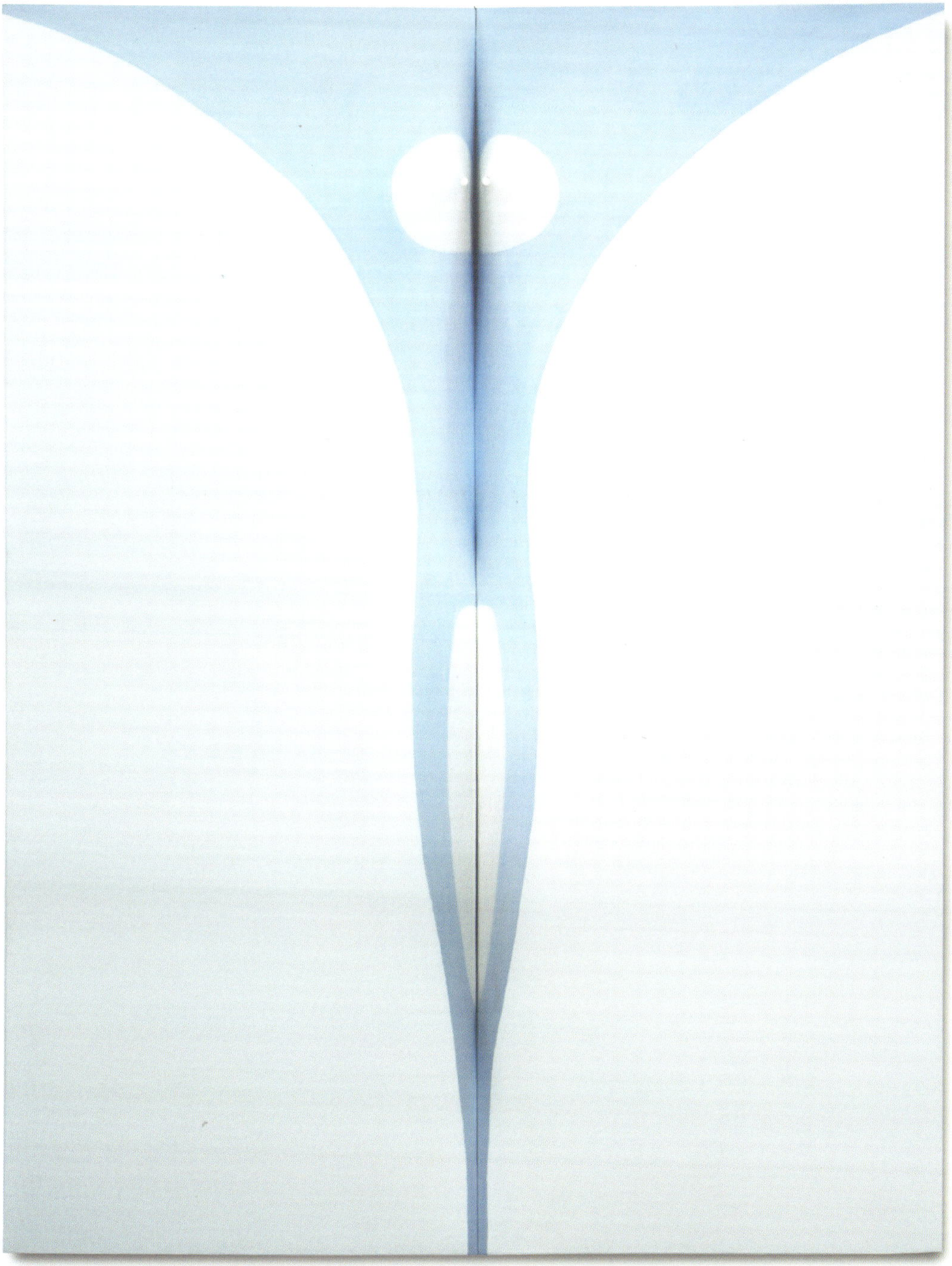

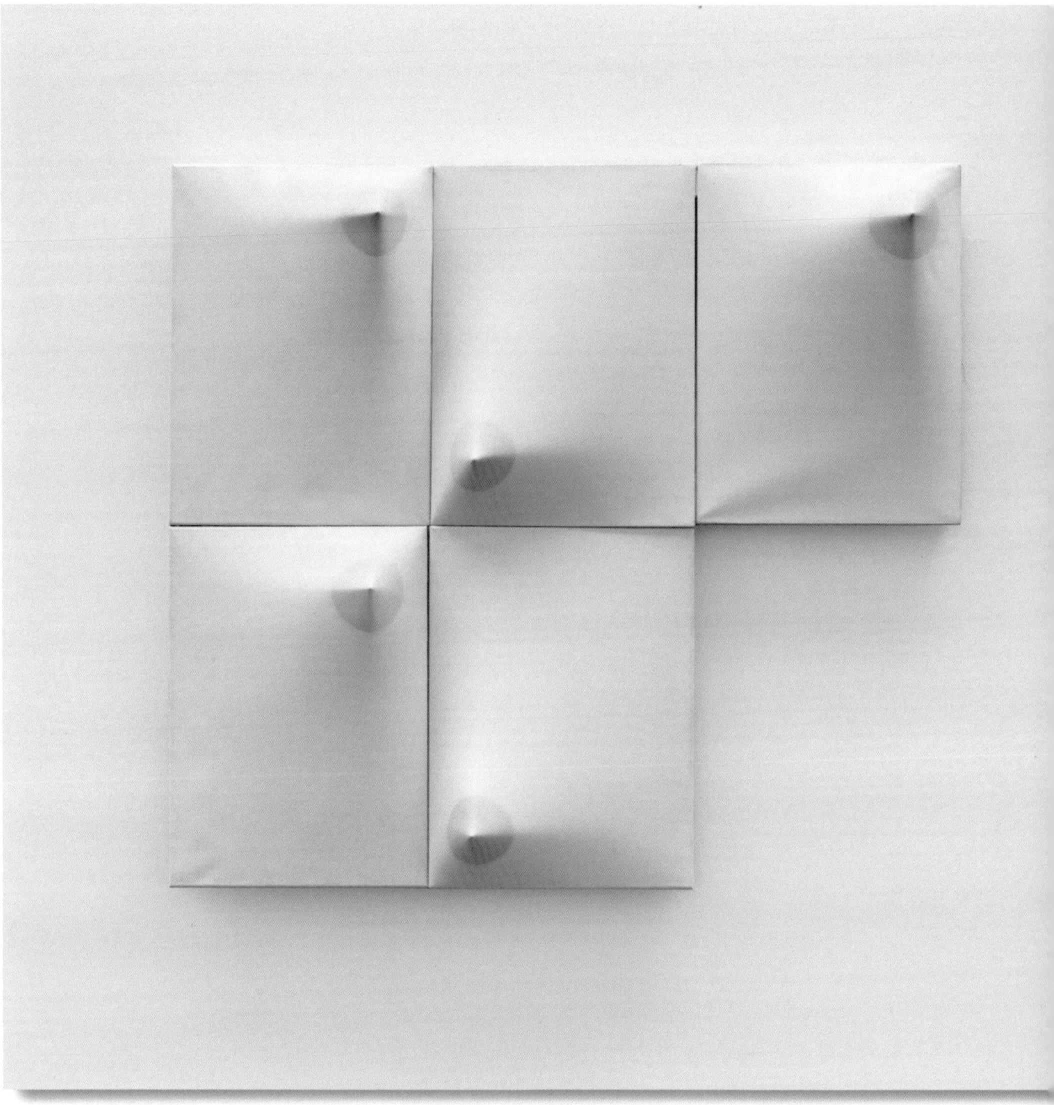

 Troyanas, políptico, 1999 | Trojans, polyptych

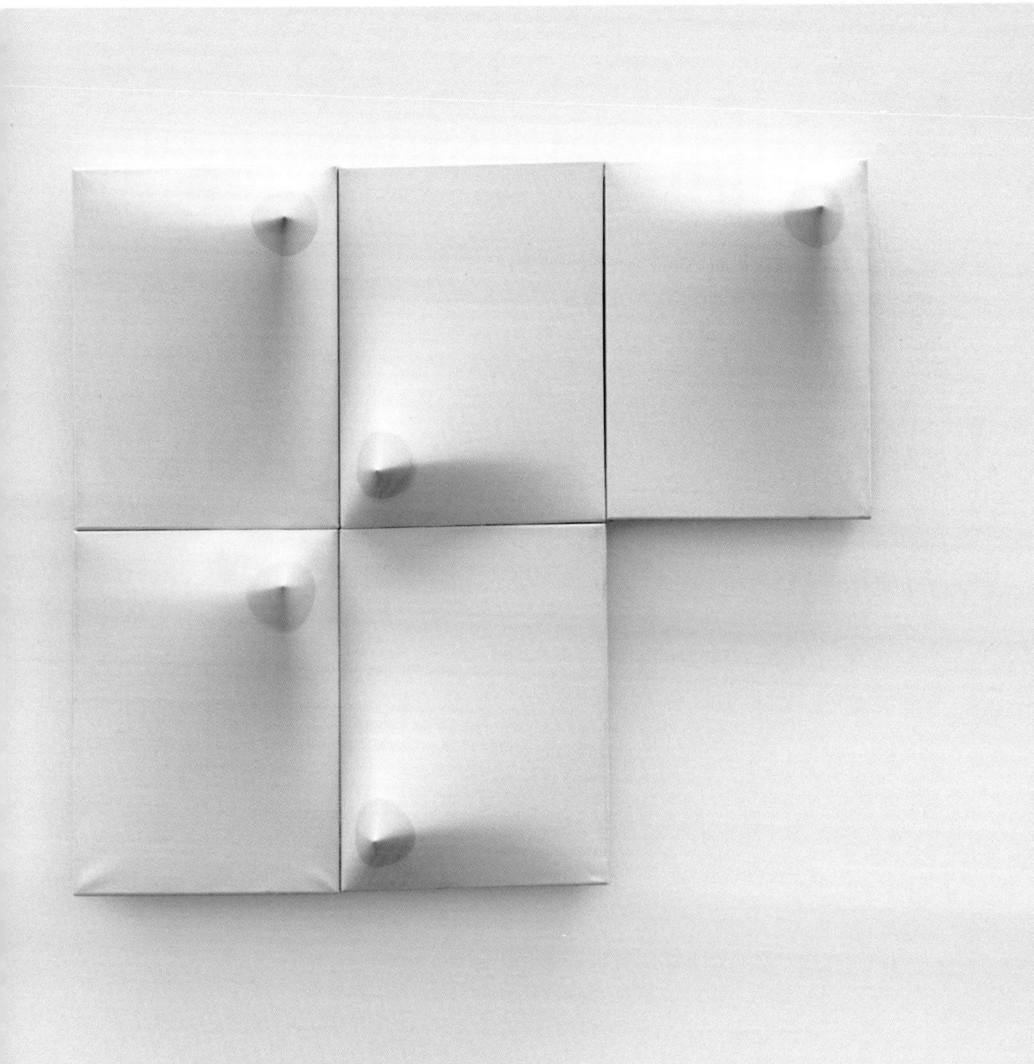

 Sin título, 1990 | Untitled

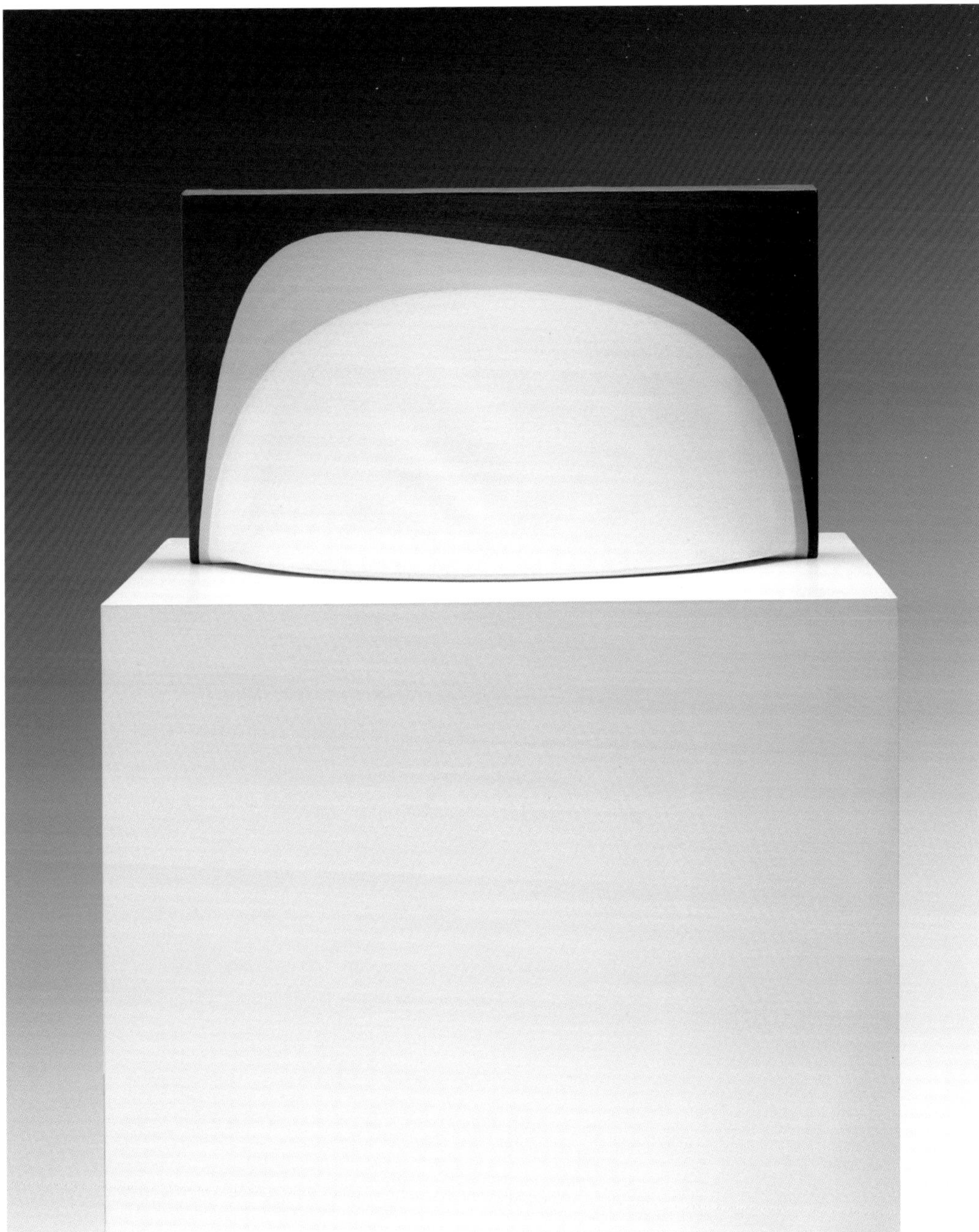

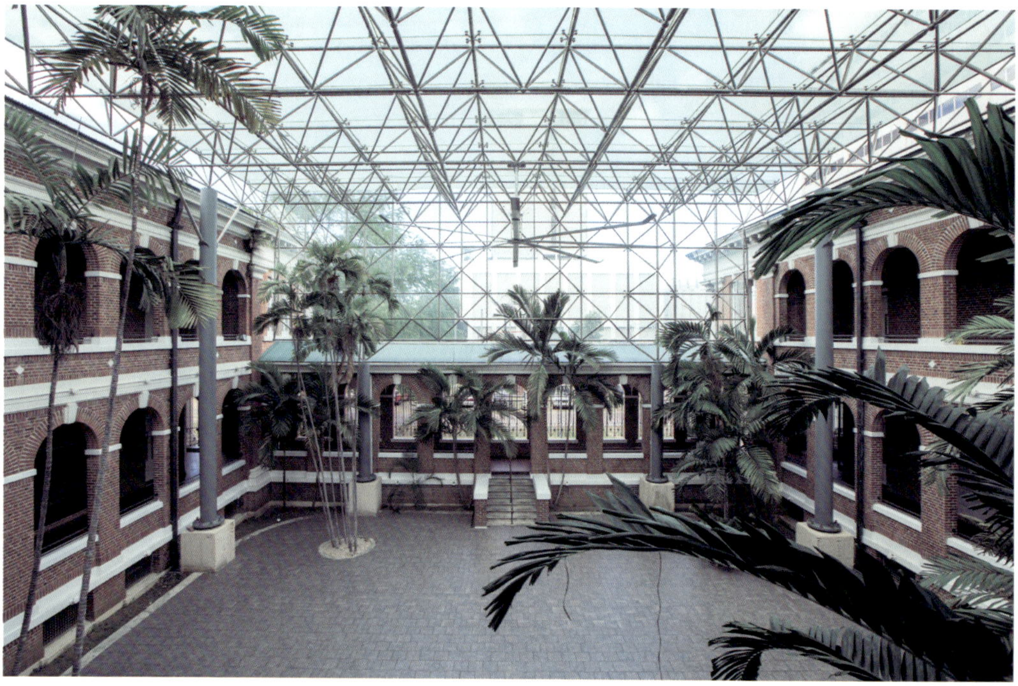

Interior courtyard of the Museo de Arte Contemporáneo de Puerto Rico, San Juan

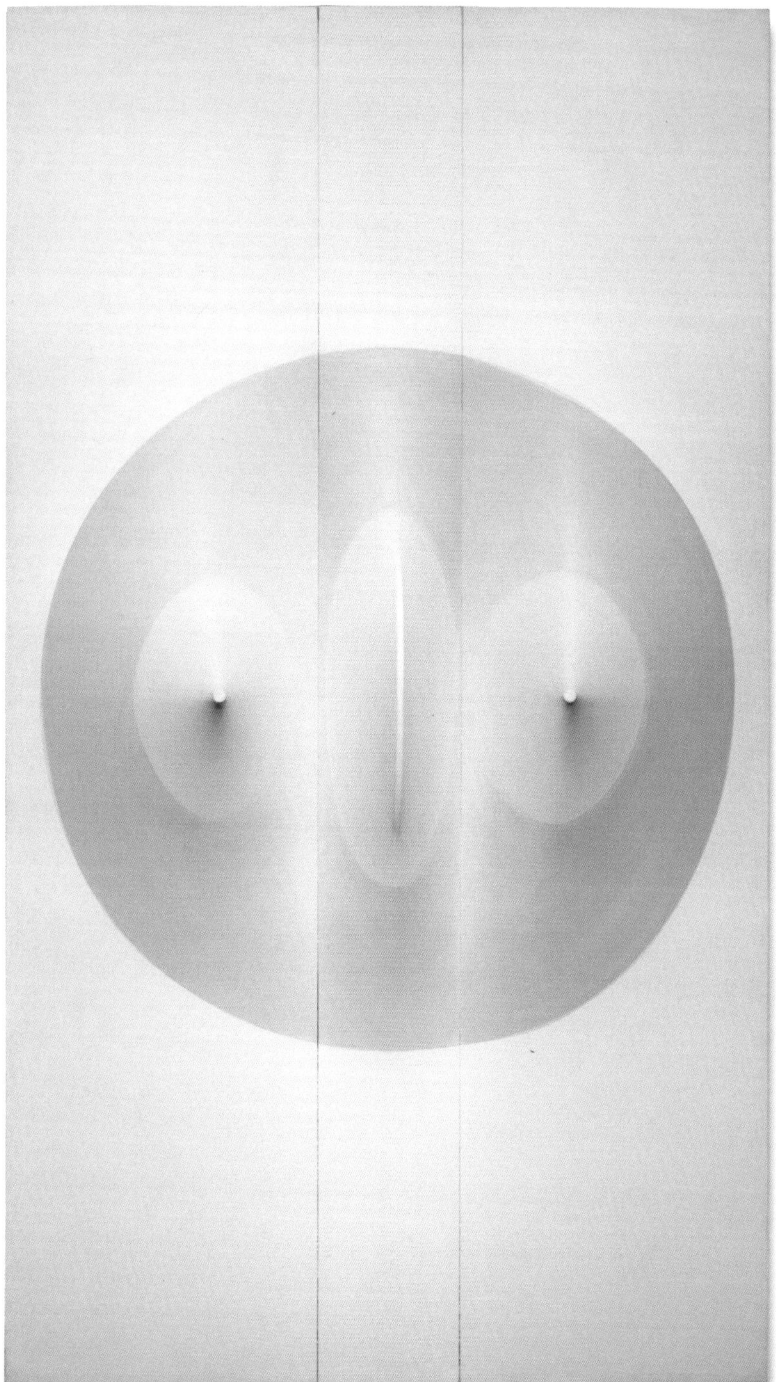

Las Amazonas, 1991 | The Amazons

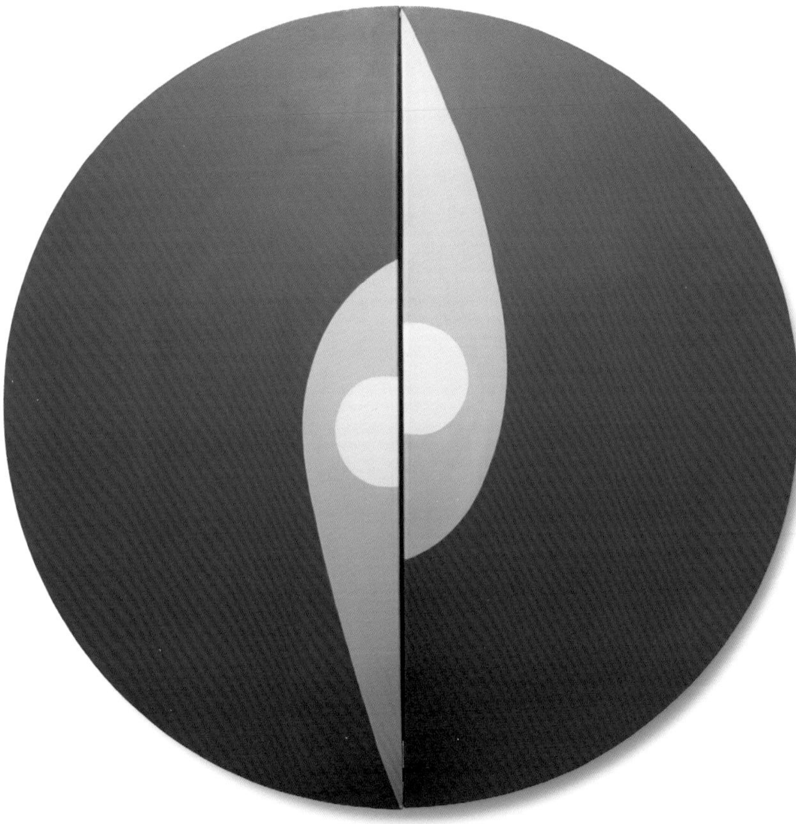

 Si yo hubiera nacido en la luna, 1993 | If I had been born on the moon

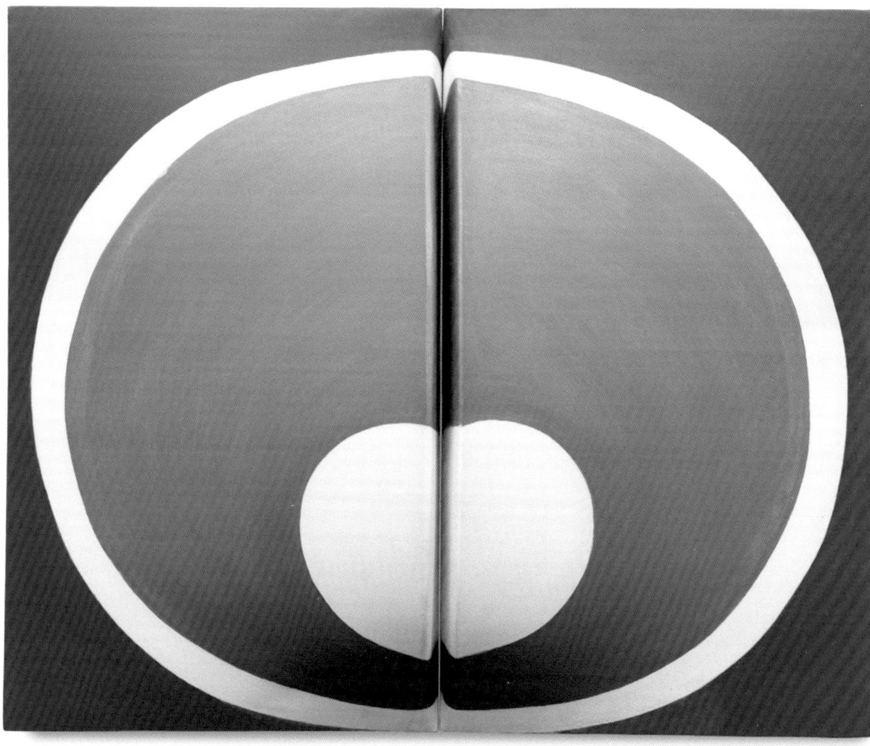

Lunar gris, negro, 1993 | Black, grey moon

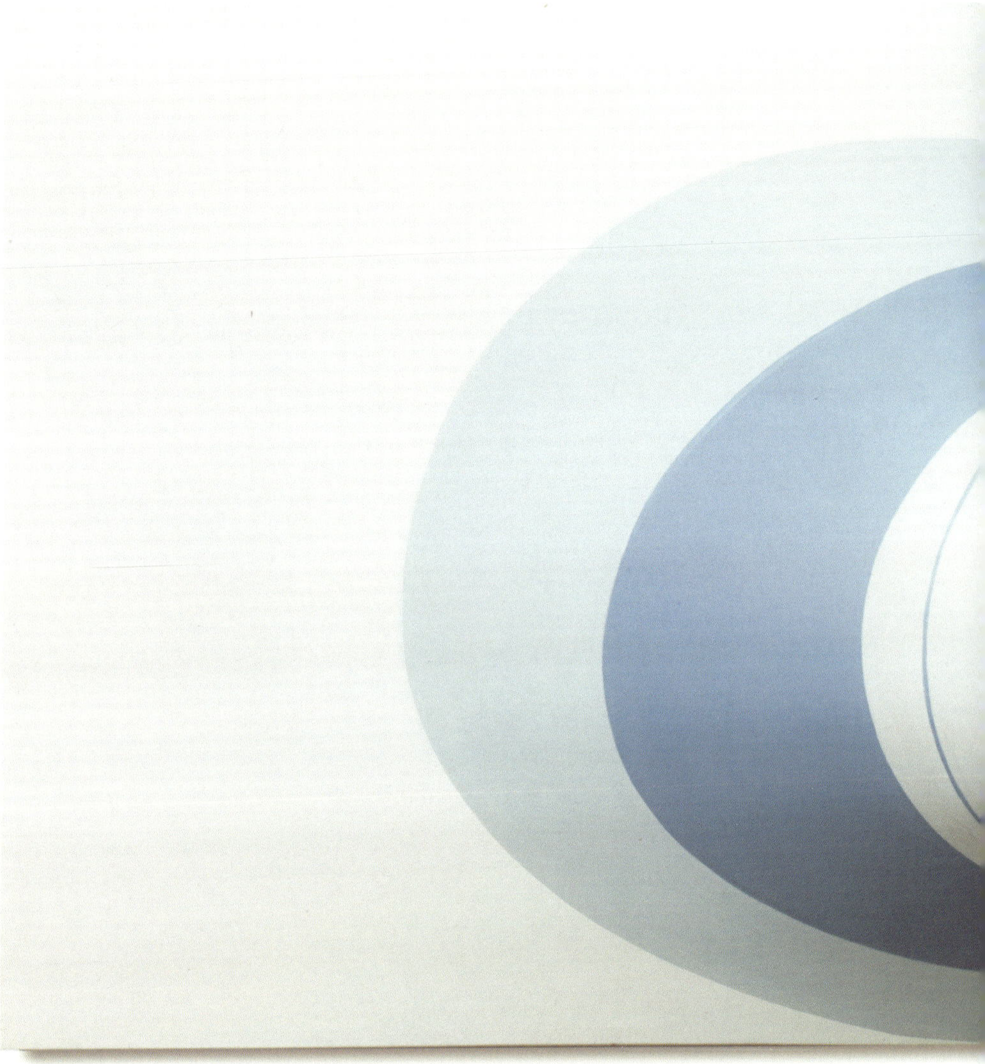

 Lunar, 1993 | Moon

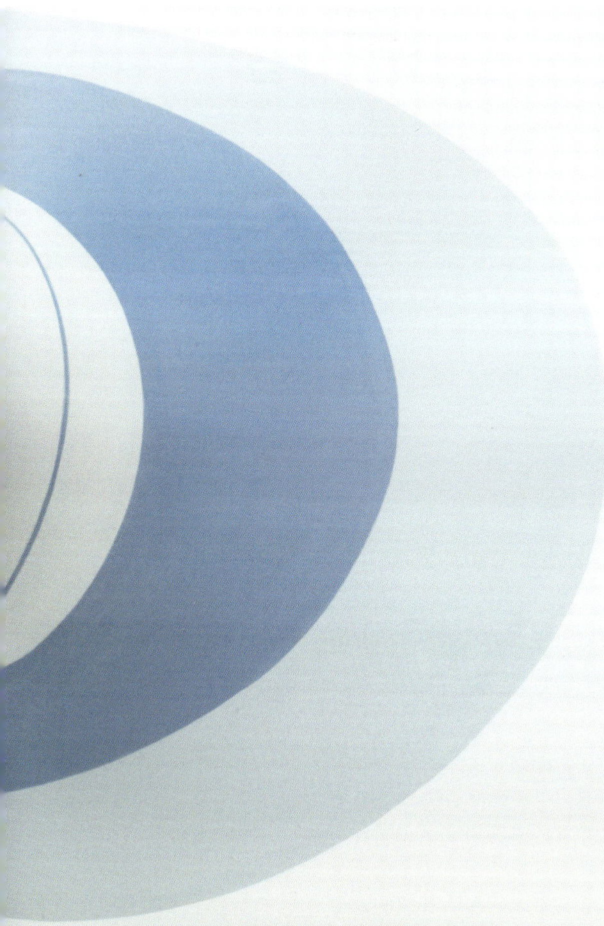

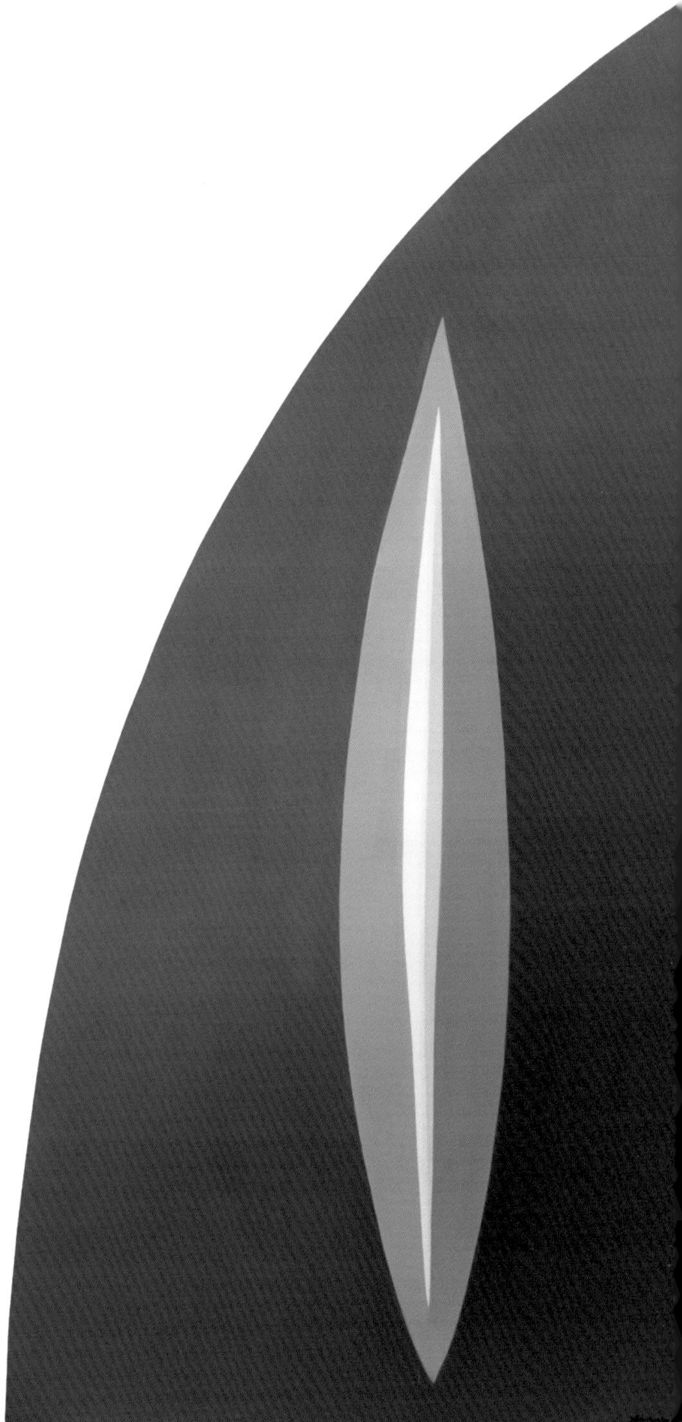

Conversatorio (de la serie Eros y la Communicación), 2014 |
Conversation (of the Eros and Communication series)

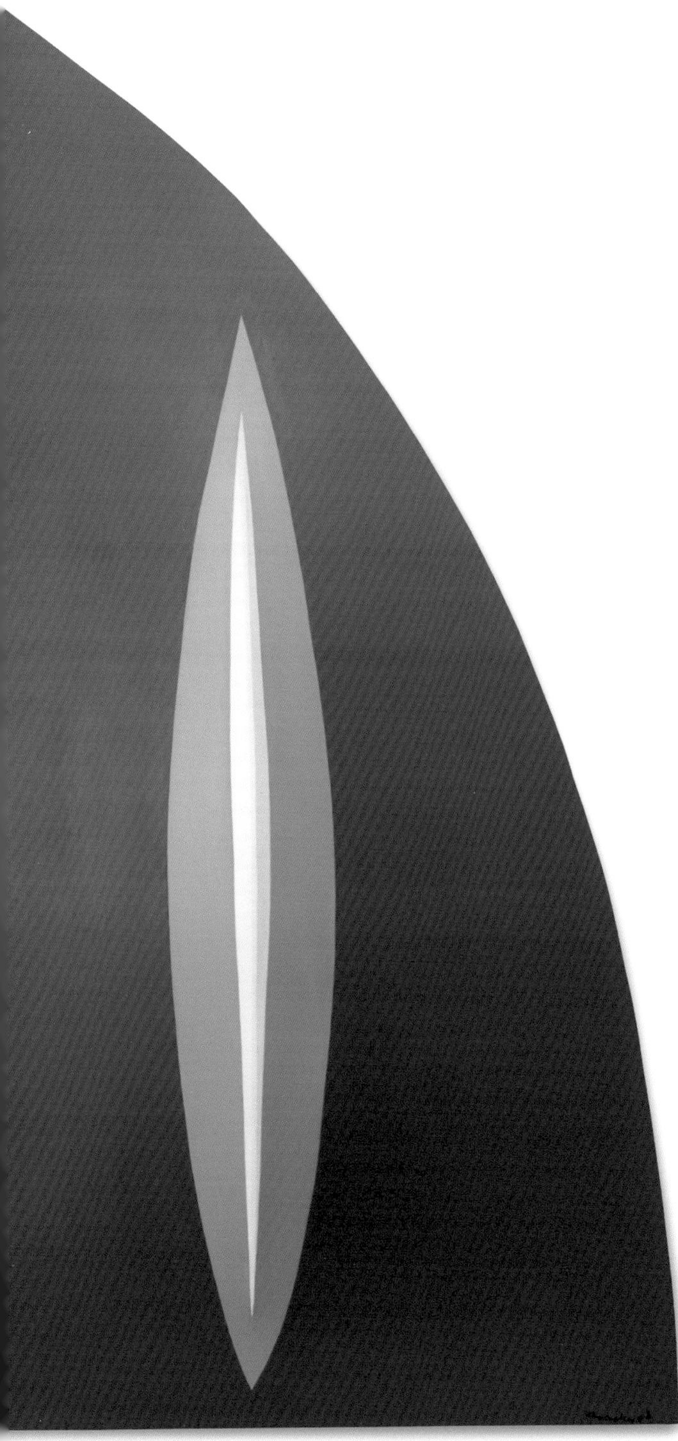

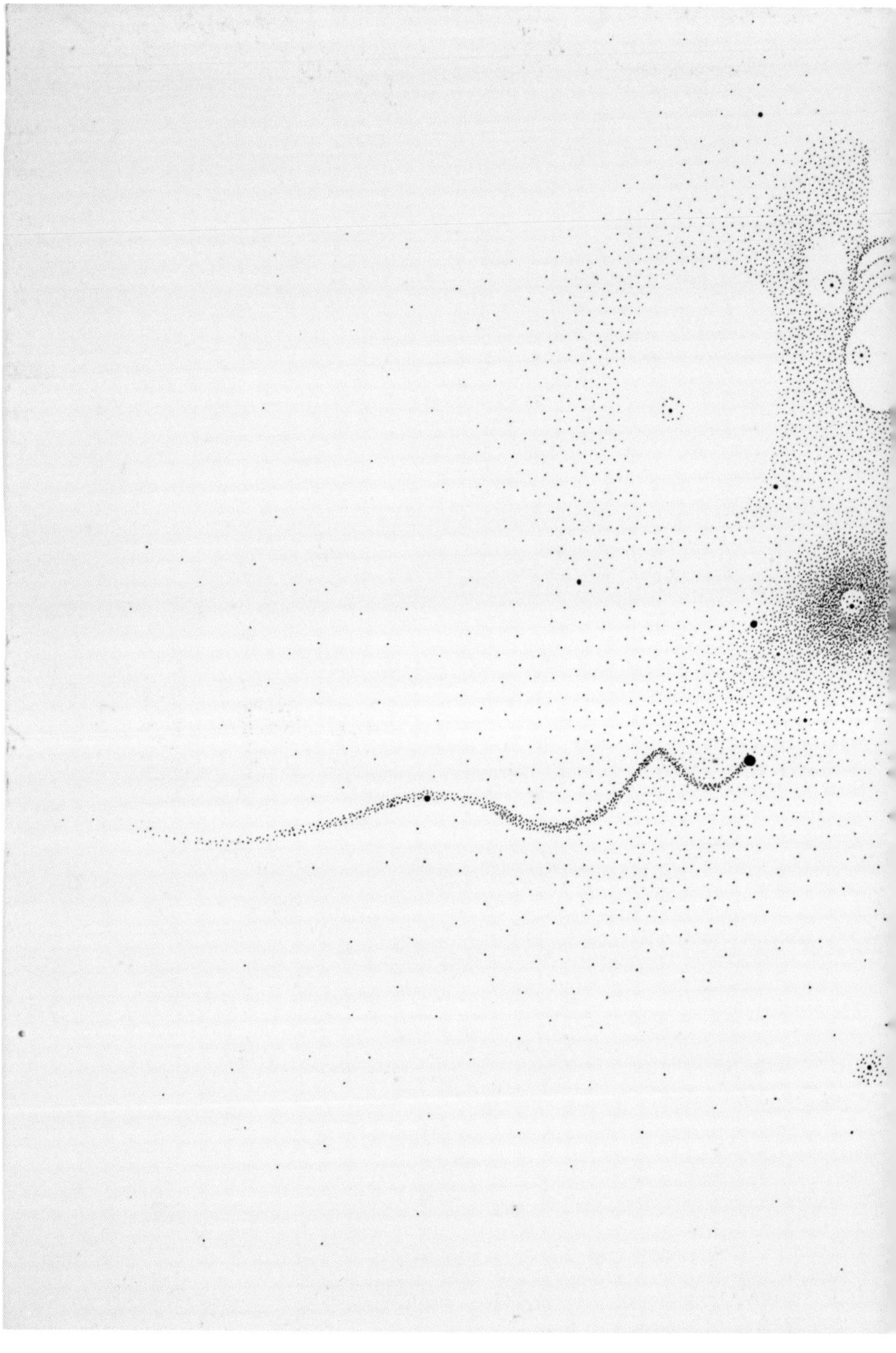

 El Significado del Significante, 1968 | The Signified of the Signifier

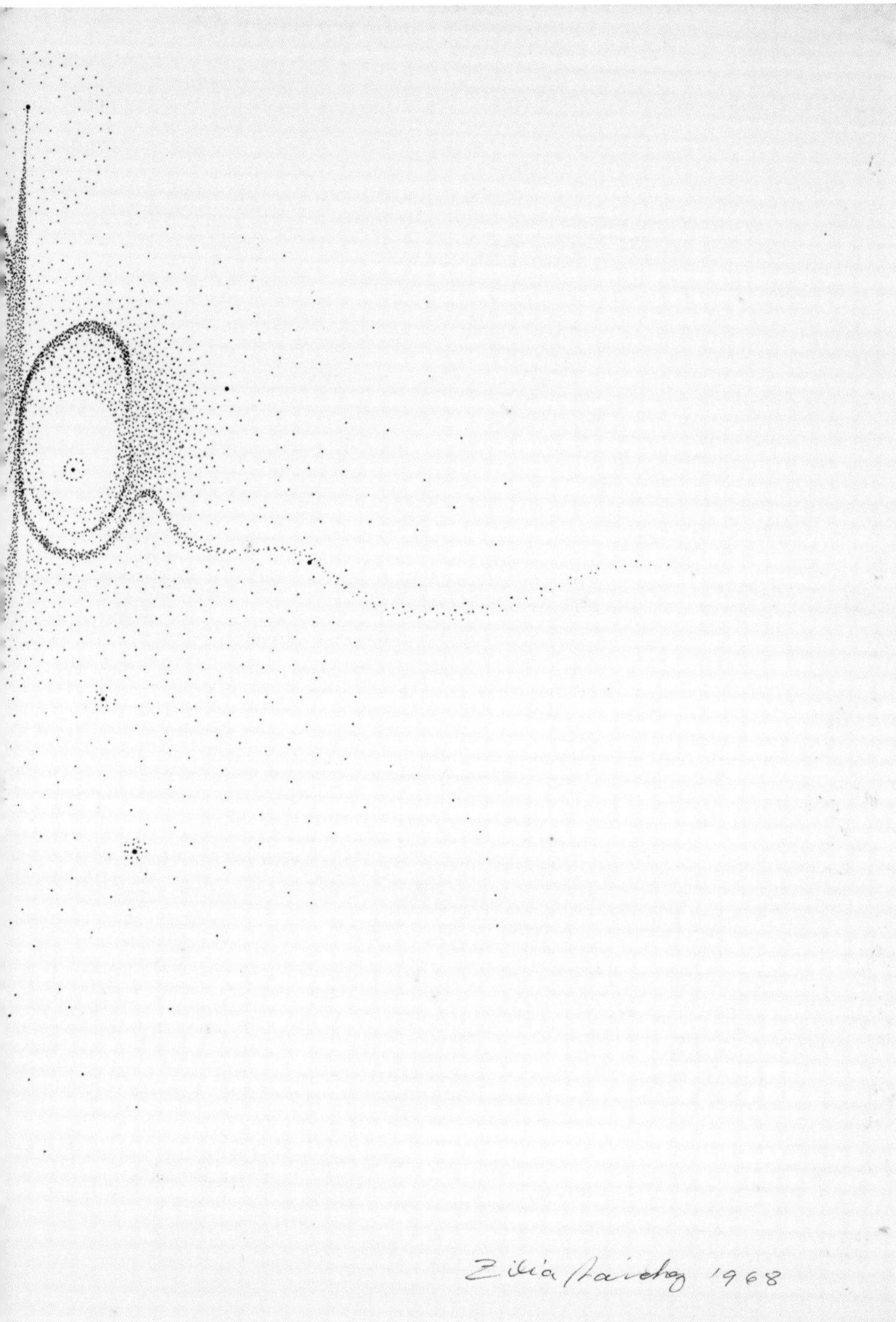
1968

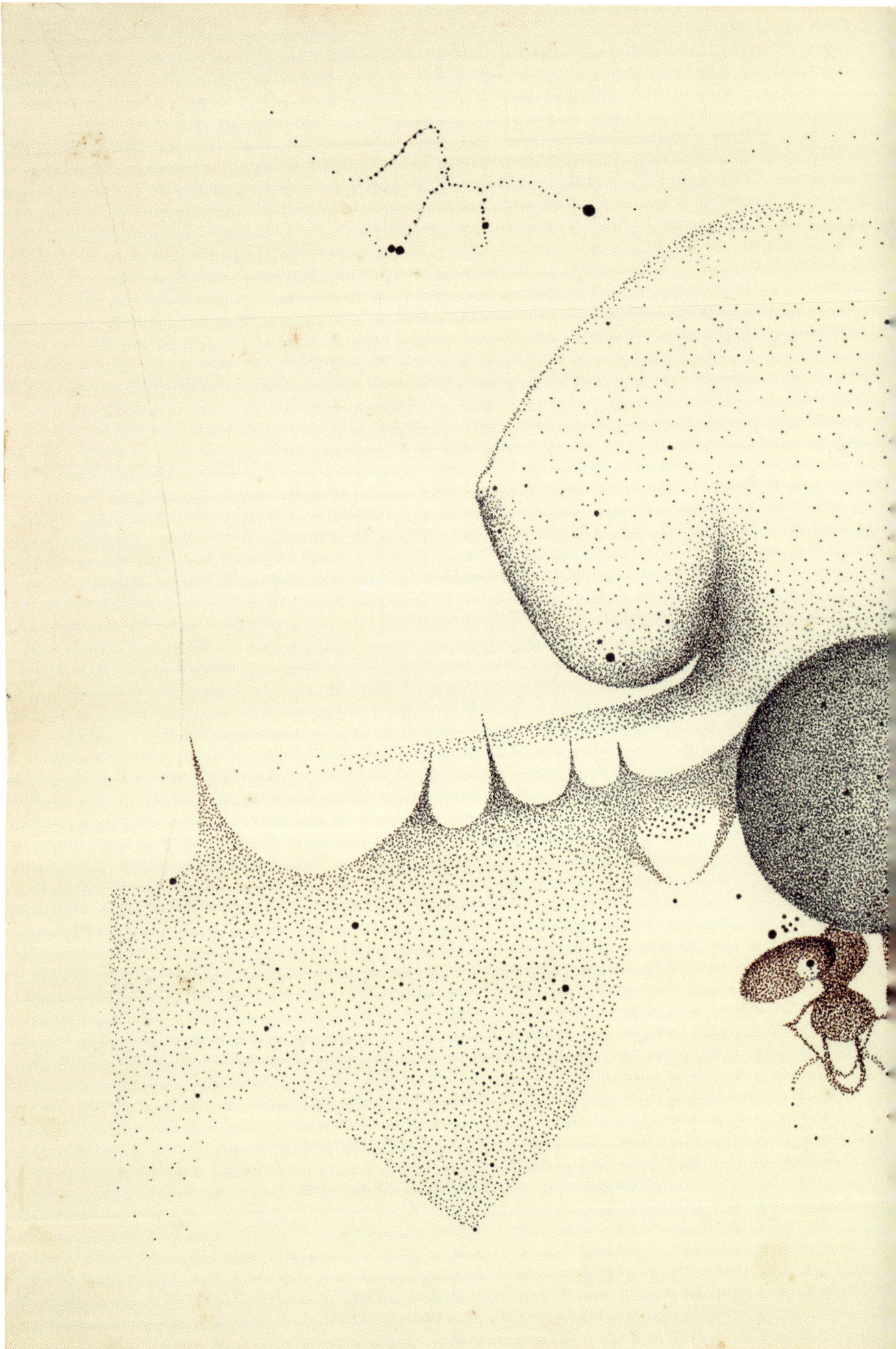

 El Significado del Significante, 1968 | The Signified of the Signifier

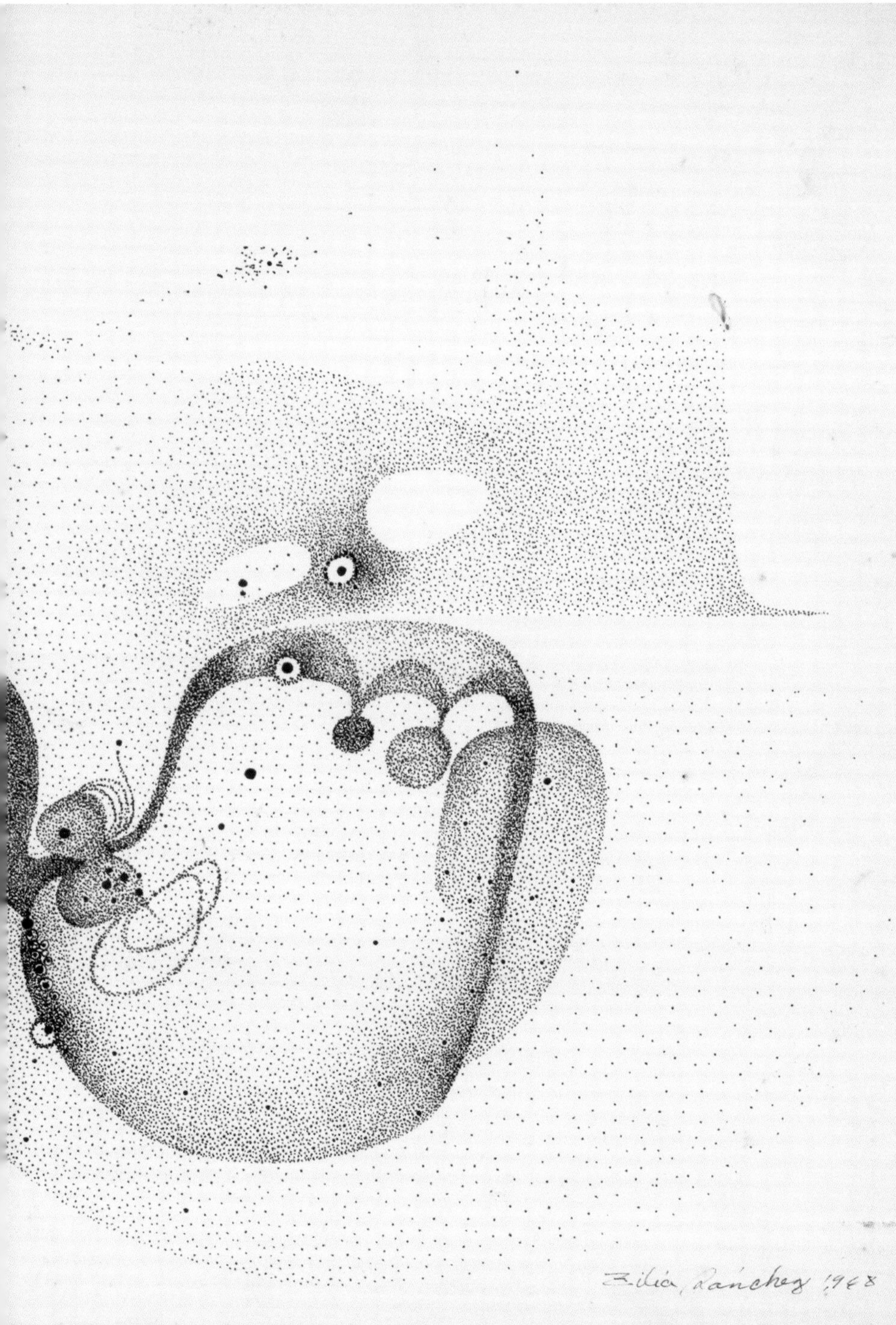
Zilia Sánchez 1968

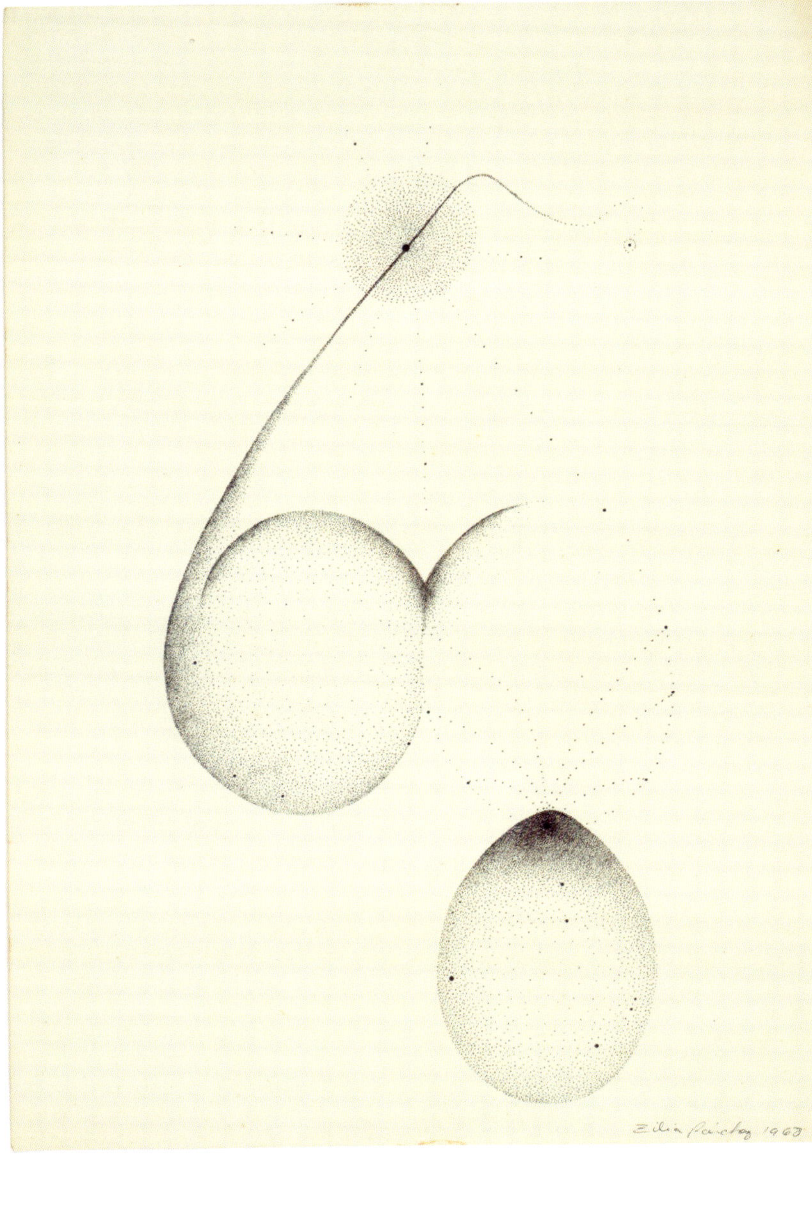

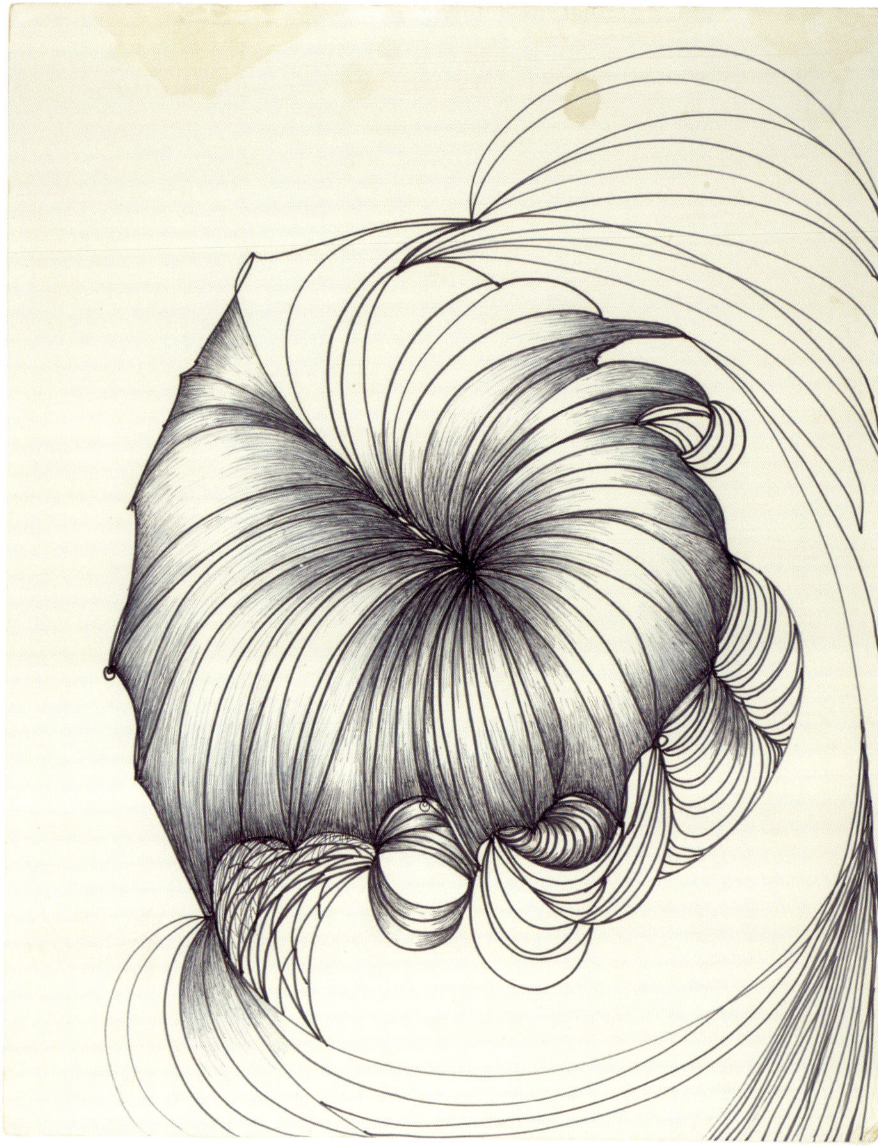

 Furia I, 1972 | Fury I

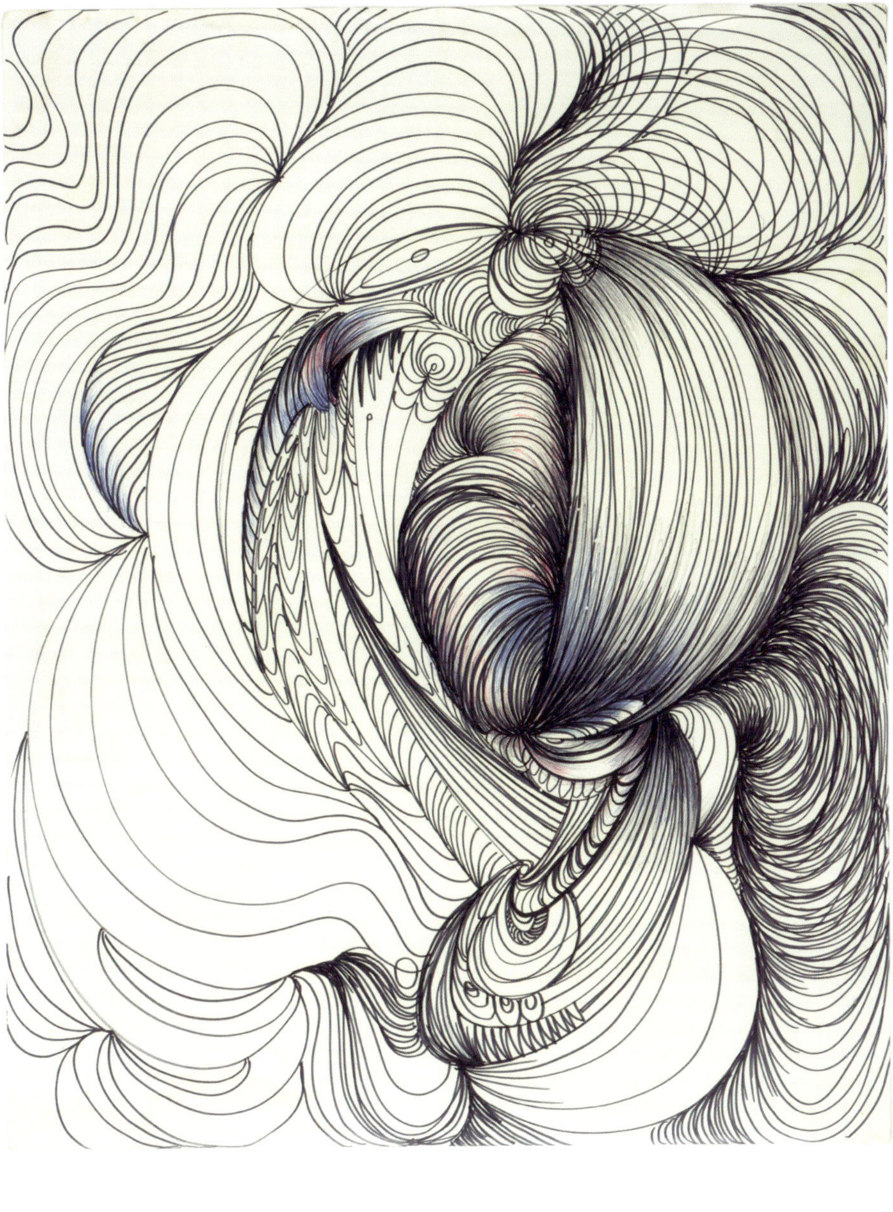

Furia II, 1972 | Fury II

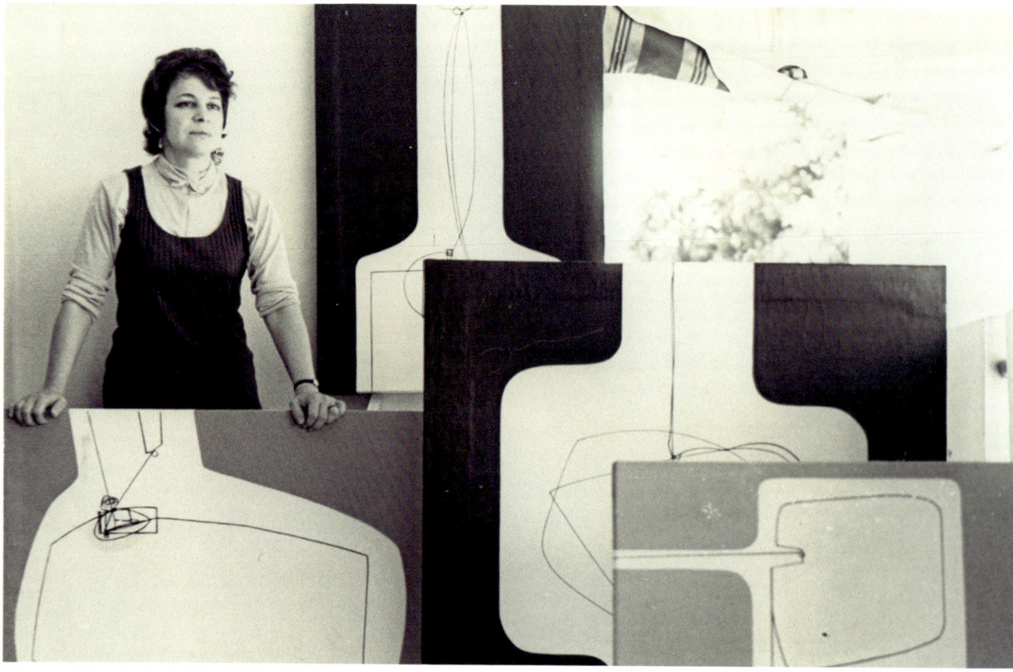

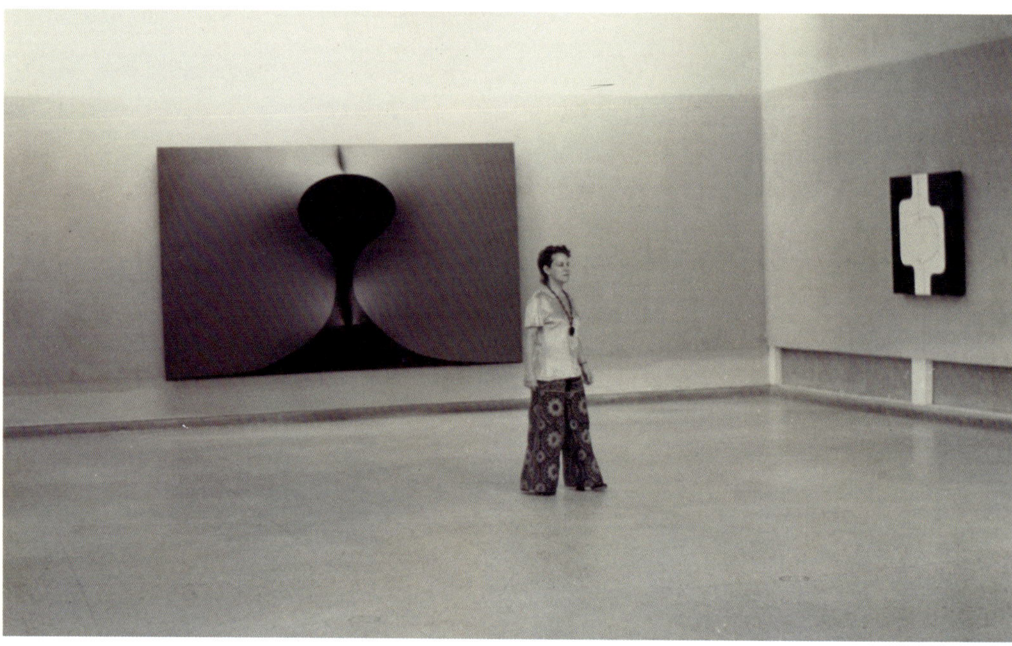

Sánchez with paintings from the *Afrocubanos (Afrocuban)* series, 1966
Installation view of *Estructuras en Secuencia* with Sánchez, 1970

Zilia Sánchez: A Chronology

Marimar Benítez

Zilia Sánchez´s extensive and multifaceted career in the visual arts includes training and practice in painting, drawing, printmaking, theatrical set design, illustration, and conservation. Born in Havana, Cuba, in 1926, Sánchez enrolled at the Havana National School of Fine Arts San Alejandro, in 1942, and earned her degree as a Professor of Drawing and Painting in 1947. In 1951 Sánchez received First Prize at the Second Romañach Painting Salon in Havana, and in 1952 she exhibited her work at the Museum of Modern Art in Paris. This opportunity was made possible by her friend and chronicler, the poet Severo Sarduy, who would also later write on Sánchez´s work in connection with various exhibitions in Cuba, Spain, and Puerto Rico.

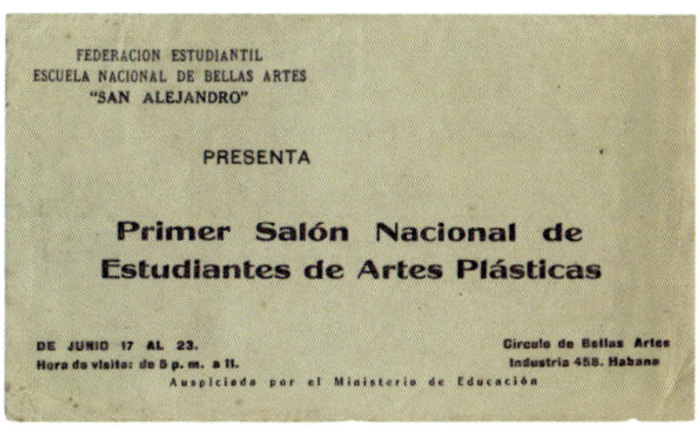

FEDERACION ESTUDIANTIL
ESCUELA NACIONAL DE BELLAS ARTES
"SAN ALEJANDRO"

PRESENTA

Primer Salón Nacional de Estudiantes de Artes Plásticas

DE JUNIO 17 AL 23.
Hora de visita: de 5 p. m. a 11.

Circulo de Bellas Artes
Industria 458. Habana

Auspiciada por el Ministerio de Educación

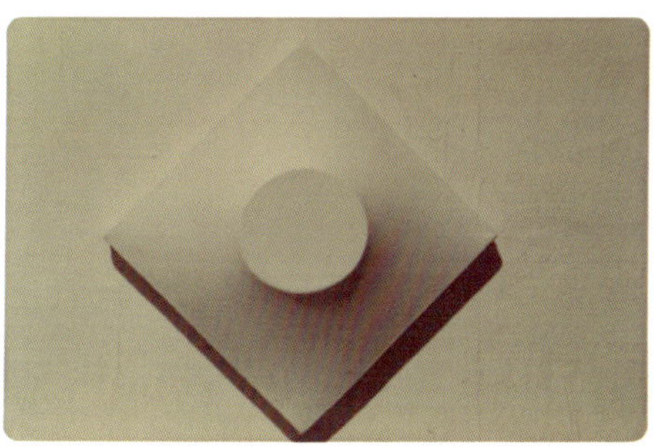

It was in her native Cuba that Zilia Sánchez gained inspiration for her signature stretched canvas works. While atop the roof of her family's home, Sánchez observed a sheet move in the wind, wrestling with roof pipes. Sánchez's first stretched canvas work was made of a piece of tubing on a tile with canvas over it, recalling the image of the sheet that would, in part, go on to shape her conception of sculptural form. Additionally, Lucio Fontana´s sliced canvases proved impactful for Sánchez; she regarded Fontana´s work as a liberating gesture that further encouraged her to pursue the stretched canvas works.

Sánchez's first solo exhibition was held at the Havana Lyceum in 1953. In 1956 Sarduy wrote the introduction to *El Tema Religioso en la Pintura Cubana*, a group exhibition at Galería Cubana in Havana. She was awarded a scholarship by the Instituto de Cultura Hispánica in Madrid in 1957, and an exhibition at Galería Clan that same year allowed for the introduction of her work to a broader,

Announcement for the *Primer Salón Nacional de Estudiantes de Artes Plásticas*, Escuela Nacional de Bellas Artes, Havana, Cuba, 1948
Sánchez's first stretched canvas painting

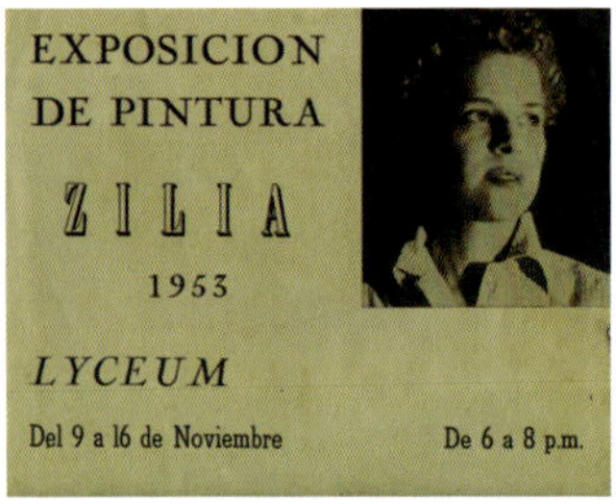

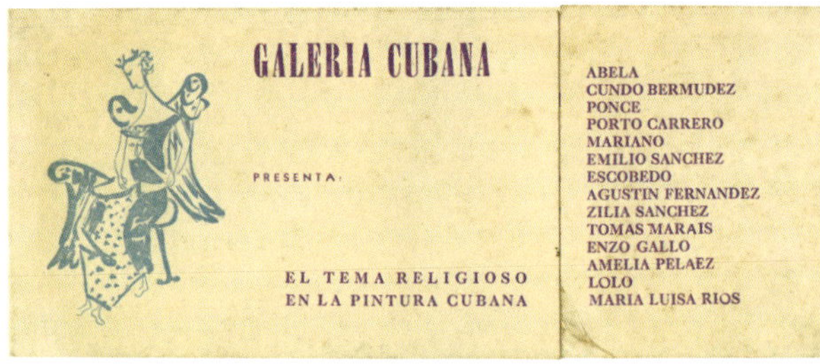

international audience. Sánchez represented Cuba in both the 1958 Bienal de México and the 1959 Bienal de São Paulo. Upon returning to Havana, she worked as a set designer for the Yesistas (Plasterers), a left-wing trade union. Later in 1959, Sánchez returned to Madrid, where she studied restoration at the Museo Nacional del Prado's Mesón del Retiro, and in 1960 she returned to Havana to work as a draftsman for the Minister of Public Works. Awarded a scholarship in 1960 to study design, Sánchez again traveled to Spain, this time to Cuenca, a thriving city for abstract art.

In 1962 Sánchez moved to New York, where she worked as an illustrator and designer for Las Americas Publishing Company and the publication *Protesta*. While in New York, Sánchez studied printmaking at Pratt Institute, and in 1965 she had her first solo show in New York at Galería Sudamericana. She exhibited paintings from the *Afrocubanos (Afrocuban)* series in a solo exhibition at the Museo de Historia, Arqueología y Arte de la Universidad de Puerto Rico in San Juan in 1966. A second solo presentation at the university museum, *Estructuras en Secuencia*, was held in 1970.

During her time abroad, Sánchez's immediate family continued to live and work in Cuba, and her relationships there remained strong and integral to her development. Sánchez's older brother, José Alberto, was the concertino of the Havana Philharmonic, and she considers her connection to Victor Manuel, a neighbor in Cuba and a mentor, instrumental to her development as an artist. Throughout the 1960s, Sánchez followed the work of Andy Warhol, Louise Nevelson, and Eva Hesse. Sánchez identified especially with Hesse in terms of both artistic production and cultural placement as women artists working within the predominantly white-male vanguard of the time.

Announcement for Sánchez's exhibition at the Havana Lyceum, 1953
Announcement for the group exhibition at Galería Cubana, 1956

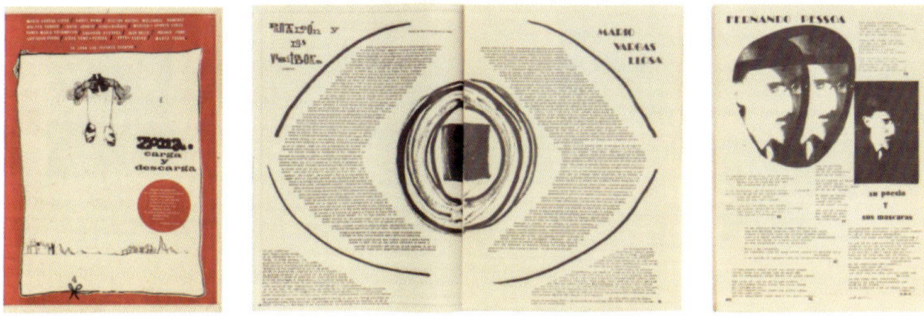

Sánchez settled in San Juan, Puerto Rico, in 1972 and began to collaborate with *Zona. Carga y Descarga*, an independent avant-garde publication by young writers. Sánchez was instrumental in establishing the distinctive design of the publication, which was based on collage and varied typographies. In 1972 Sánchez exhibited at the Palacio de Bellas Artes in Caracas, Venezuela, while continuing to teach at the San Juan Art Students League and the Escuela de Artes Plásticas.

In 1980 Sánchez was awarded First Prize at the Biennial in Medellín, Colombia. During the 1980s and 1990s she continued to exhibit, primarily in Puerto Rico as well as the contiguous United States. In 1999 Sánchez presented as part of a group exhibition at the Fundació Joan Miró in Barcelona. In 2000 Sánchez exhibited *Heróicas Eróticas* at the Museo de las Américas in San Juan. Her 2013 exhibition at Artists Space in New York was considered "one of the year's high points, a revelation and a refreshment" by Holland Cotter of the *New York Times.* In 2014 the International Art Critics Association (AICA), Puerto Rico Chapter, awarded Sánchez a prize for Best Exhibition by a Puerto Rican Artist Abroad for this exhibition. Galerie Lelong New York began representing Sánchez in 2013.

Zilia Sánchez, age 87, continues to work in San Juan, Puerto Rico.

Professor Marimar Benítez is the current President of the International Art Critics Association (AICA), Puerto Rico Chapter. She has devoted her professional career to studying and promoting the visual arts of Puerto Rico. She has served as Registrar and Visiting Curator at the Museo de Arte de Ponce, and the Curator of Collections at the Instituto de Cultura Puertorriqueña. From 1993 to 2011 she was the Chancellor of the Escuela de Artes Plásticas de Puerto Rico.

Zona. Carga y Descarga, Issue 4, March-April 1973
Editor and Publisher: Rosario Ferré. Design and Photomontage: Zilia Sánchez

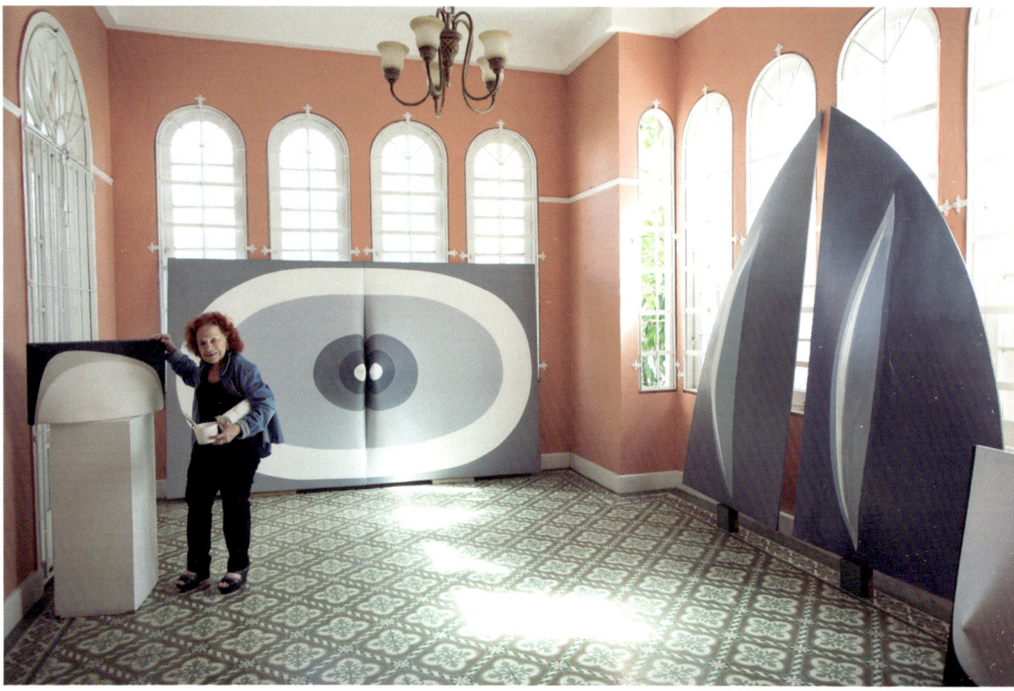

 Sánchez in her studio, 2014

Zilia Sánchez

Born 1926, Havana, Cuba
Lives and works in San Juan, Puerto Rico

Escuela Nacional de Bellas Artes San Alejandro, Havana, Cuba, 1947

Selected Solo Exhibitions

2014 *Heróicas Eróticas en Nueva York*, Galerie Lelong, New York, New York
2013 Artists Space, New York, New York
2009 *Construcciones en Secuencia*, Casa Sofia, San Juan, Puerto Rico
2000 *Heróicas Eróticas,* Museo de las Américas, San Juan, Puerto Rico
1991 *Tres Décadas,* Museo Casa Roig, Humacao, Puerto Rico
1984 *Erótica,* Intar Latin American Gallery, New York, New York
1980 Liga de Estudiantes de Arte de San Juan, San Juan, Puerto Rico
1973 Exhibition at the residence of Dr. Marrero, San Juan, Puerto Rico
1971 Arts Center Museum, Miami, Florida
1970 *Estructuras en Secuencia,* Museo de Historia, Arqueología y Arte de la Universidad de Puerto Rico, San Juan, Puerto Rico
Palacio de Bellas Artes, Caracas, Venezuela
Metaphoric Visualizations of Reality, Western Maryland College, Westminster, Maryland
Structures and Prints, Sarduy Gallery, New York, New York
1968 Instituto Catalán de Cultura Hispánica, Barcelona, Spain
1967 Galería El Bosco, Madrid, Spain
1966 Museo de Historia, Arqueología y Arte de la Universidad de Puerto Rico, San Juan, Puerto Rico
Zegri Gallery, New York, New York
1965 Galería Sudamericana, New York, New York
1958 Museo Nacional de Bellas Artes de La Habana, Havana, Cuba
Scenography for *Las Máscaras*, Teatro de los Yesistas, Havana, Cuba
1957 *Exposición de Pinturas, Zilia Sánchez*, Galería Clan, Madrid, Spain
Galería Cubana, Havana, Cuba
1956 Galería Cubana, Havana, Cuba
1953 Lyceum, Havana, Cuba

Selected Group Exhibitions

2014 *To Whom Does the World Belong?*, El Museo del Barrio, New York, New York

Looking Back: The 8th White Columns Annual, White Columns, New York, New York

2008 *Circa of Puerto Rico*, Feria de Arte Centro de Convenciones, San Juan, Puerto Rico

2006 *Solo*, CIRCA, Puerto Rico

1999 Fundació Joan Miró, Barcelona, Spain

1998 *100 Años después*, Instituto de Cultura Puertorriqueña, San Juan, Puerto Rico

Pequeño Formato, Museo de las Américas, San Juan, Puerto Rico

Artistas Contra el Sida, Fundación Sida de Puerto Rico, San Juan, Puerto Rico

1997 Fort Lauderdale Museum of Art, Fort Lauderdale, Florida

Museo de Arte Contemporáneo de Puerto Rico, San Juan, Puerto Rico

Galería de la Escuela de Artes Plásticas, San Juan, Puerto Rico

Museo de las Américas, San Juan, Puerto Rico

Exposición de la Facultad de la Escuela de Artes Plásticas, Museo de Historia, Arqueología y Arte de la Universidad de Puerto Rico, San Juan, Puerto Rico

1992 *Exhibición Conmemorativa Vigésimoquinto Aniversario,* Sala de Exposiciones de Citibank, Cupey, Puerto Rico

1990 *Colectiva de Profesores*, Liga de Estudiantes de Arte de San Juan, San Juan, Puerto Rico

Mujeres Artistas: Protagonistas de los Ochenta, Museo de las Casas Reales, Santo Domingo, Dominican Republic. Traveled to Museo de Arte Contemporáneo de Puerto Rico, San Juan, Puerto Rico

1987 *Out of Cuba*, Rutgers University, New Brunswick, New Jersey. Traveled to University of Miami, Miami, Florida

Museo de Arte Moderno La Tertulia VI Biennial, Medellín, Colombia

1985 *Veinticinco Años de Pintura Puertorriqueña*, Museo de Arte de Ponce, Ponce, Puerto Rico

Semana de la Mujer, Plaza las Américas, San Juan, Puerto Rico

1984 Lehigh University, Bethlehem, Pennsylvania

Galería Luigi Marrozzini, San Juan, Puerto Rico

Primer Congreso de Artistas Abstractos de Puerto Rico, Arsenal de la Puntilla del Instituto de Cultura Puertorriqueña, San Juan, Puerto Rico

Séptimo Salón de la UNESCO, San Juan, Puerto Rico

Pontiac Creative Arts Center, Pontiac, Michigan

1983 *Women Artists from Puerto Rico*, Cayman Gallery, New York, New York
Arte Actual: Puerto Rico, Liga de Estudiantes de Arte de San Juan, Chase Manhattan Bank, San Juan, Puerto Rico
1982 *Obra Puertorriqueña de Artistas Cubanos,* San Juan, Puerto Rico
Semana de la Mujer, Plaza las Américas, San Juan, Puerto Rico
1981 Salón Anual del Instituto de Cultura, San Juan, Puerto Rico
Liga de Estudiantes de Arte, San Juan, Puerto Rico
1980 Museo de Arte Moderno La Tertulia I Biennial, Medellín, Colombia
1978 Liga de Estudiantes de Arte, San Juan, Puerto Rico
1975 *Cuatro Pintoras y una Escultora,* Galería María Rechany, San Juan, Puerto Rico
1974 *Arte Latinoamericano,* Galería las Américas, San Juan, Puerto Rico
1972 Segunda Bienal de Grabado Latinoamericano, San Juan, Puerto Rico
Exposición de Pintura Cubana, Palacio de Bellas Artes, Caracas, Venezuela
Reencuentro de la Pintura Cubana, Arts Center Museum, Miami, Florida
1970 Bienal de Grabado Latinoamericano, San Juan, Puerto Rico
Catorce Pintores Latinoamericanos, The Staff Association of the Inter-American Development Bank, Washington, DC
1969 *Modern Painters in New York*, Herbert E. Feist Gallery, New York, New York
Cuban Painting in New York, Sarduy Gallery, New York, New York
Pintores Latinoamericanos en San Juan, Galería Alegría, San Juan, Puerto Rico
Museo de Bellas Artes, Dirección de Cultura, Havana, Cuba
1968 *Exposición de Pintura Latinoamericana,* Zegri Gallery, New York, New York
1966 Park Gallery, New Jersey
Galería Sudamericana, New York, New York
La Casa del Arte, San Juan, Puerto Rico
1959 Quinto São Paulo Biennial, São Paulo, Brazil
1958 Bienal de México, Museo Nacional de Artes Plásticas, Mexico City, Mexico
Asociación de Reporteros, Caracas, Venezuela
1957 Barquisimeto Commerce Club, Barquisimeto, Caracas, Venezuela
1956 *VIII Salón Nacional de Dirección de Cultura: Exposición de Cuatro Pintoras Cubanas: Amelia Peláez, Mirta Cerra, María Luisa Ríos y Zilia Sánchez,* Instituto Nacional de Cultura, Ministerio de Educación, Havana, Cuba
Homenaje a G.V. Pérez Cisneros, Cuba
El Tema Religioso en la Pintura Cubana, Galería Cubana, Havana, Cuba
1955 *Exposición en Homenaje a Luis de Soto,* Sociedad Nuestro Tiempo, Havana, Cuba
1954 Universidad de la Habana, Lyceum de la Habana, Havana, Cuba
Misión Gubernamental, Madrid, Spain
1953 *VI Salón de Pintura y Escultura*, Salones del Capitolio Nacional, Havana, Cuba
1952 Sociedad de Nuestro Tiempo, Havana, Cuba
Museum of Modern Art, Paris, France

1951 Segundo Salón Romañach, Havana, Cuba
1950 *IV Exposición Nacional de Pintura, Escultura y Grabado*, Ministerio de Educacion, Centro Asturiano, Havana, Cuba
1948 *Primer Salón Nacional de Estudiantes de Artes Plásticas*, Escuela Nacional de Bellas Artes, Havana, Cuba
1947 *II Salón de Otoño*, Liceo artístico y literario de Regla, Havana, Cuba

Awards and Fellowships

2014 Best Exhibition by a Puerto Rican Artist Abroad: Zilia Sánchez at Artists Space in New York, The International Art Critics Association (AICA), San Juan, Puerto Rico
1987 Acquisitions Prize, Museo de Arte Moderno La Tertulia VI Biennial, Medellín, Colombia
1986 Excellence Award, Metro Art Gallery, New York, New York
1980 Press First Prize, Museo de Arte Moderno La Tertulia I Biennial, Medellín, Colombia
1978 First Prize, Cuarto Salón de Pintura de UNESCO, San Juan, Puerto Rico
1968 Cintas Foundation Award, New York, New York
1966 Cintas Foundation Award, New York, New York
1959 Instituto de Cultura Hispánica, Madrid, Spain
1951 First Prize, Second Romañach Painting Salon, Havana, Cuba

Public Collections

Instituto de Cultura Hispánica, Madrid, Spain
Instituto de Cultura Puertorriqueña, San Juan, Puerto Rico
Miami Dade College, Miami, Florida
Ministerio de Educación, Havana, Cuba
Museo de Arte Contemporáneo de Puerto Rico, San Juan, Puerto Rico
Museo de Arte de Ponce, Ponce, Puerto Rico
Museo de Arte de Puerto Rico, San Juan, Puerto Rico

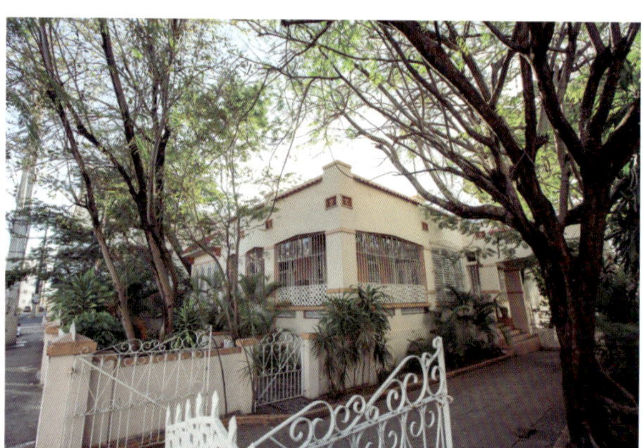

Sánchez's studio in San Juan, Puerto Rico

List of Plate Illustrations

All works included in the exhibition unless otherwise noted.

* indicates not included in the exhibition.

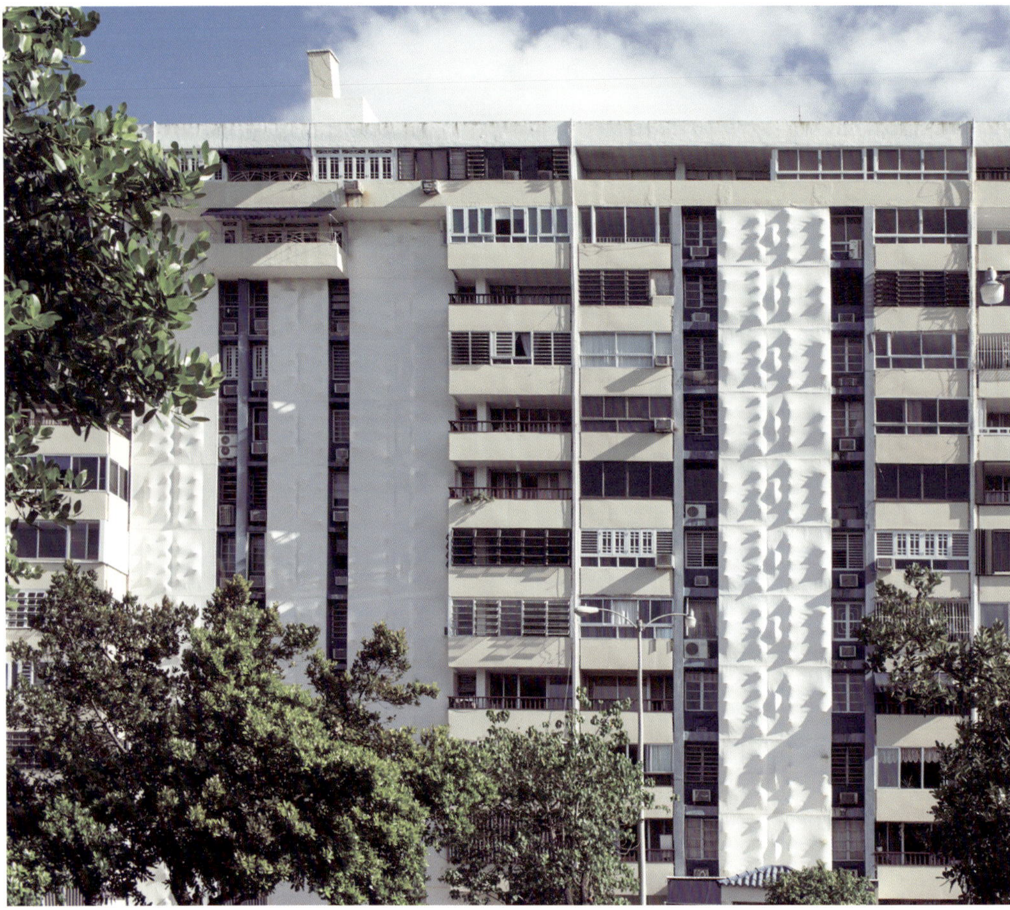

Sánchez's monumental work in concrete, created in 1971,
on the facade of apartment buildings in Laguna Gardens, San Juan, Puerto Rico

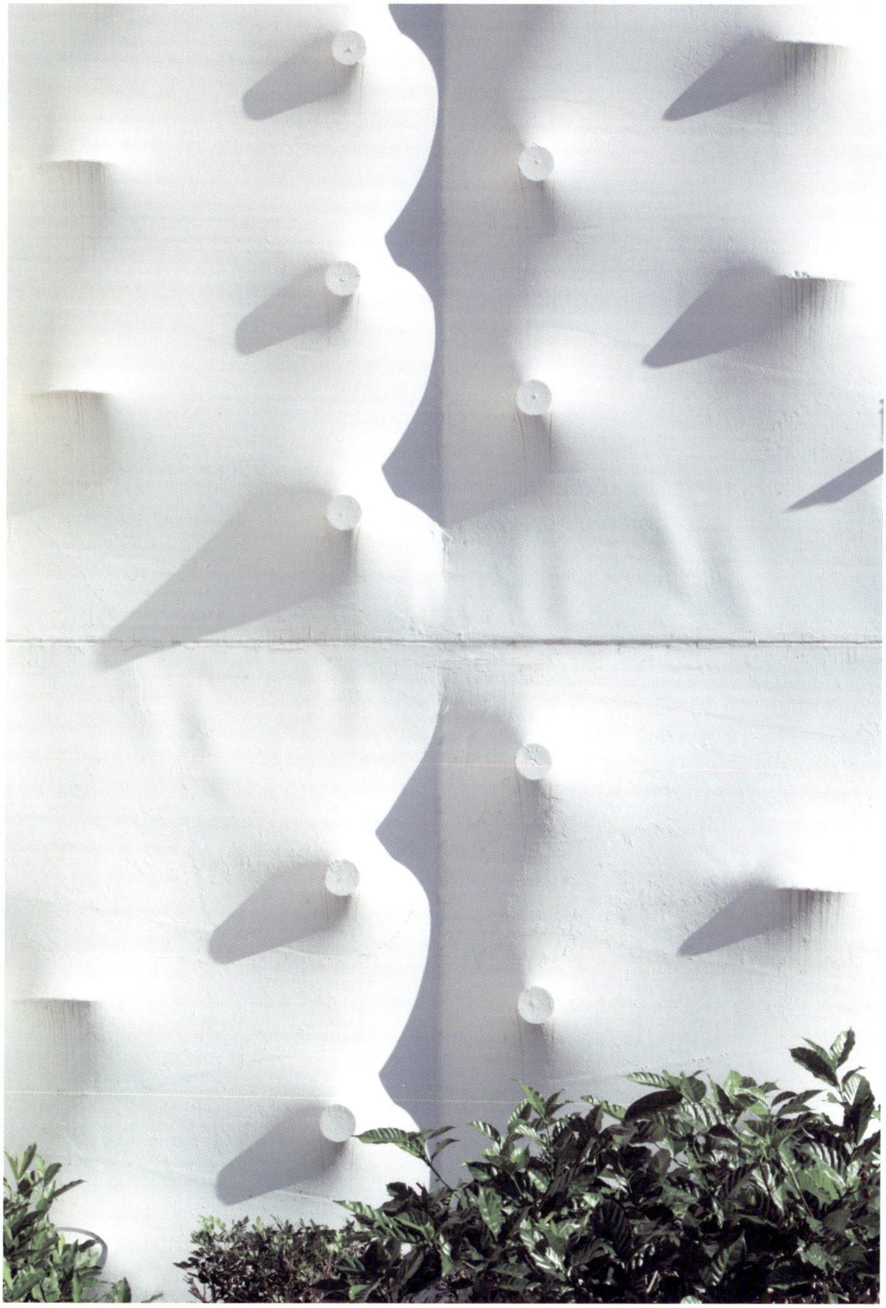

Published in conjunction with the exhibition:

Zilia Sánchez
Heróicas Eróticas en Nueva York
May 3 - June 21, 2014
Galerie Lelong, New York

Published by:
Actar Publishers and Galerie Lelong

Galerie Lelong
528 West 26th Street
New York, NY 10001
www.galerielelong.com

Actar D
151 Grand St, Fl 5
New York, NY 10013
www. actar-d.com

Book Coordination:
Sarah Landry
Maria Heinz

Texts:
Irene V. Small
Marimar Benítez

Photographs:
Michael Bodycomb
Raquel Pérez Puig
Daniel Pérez

Cover:
Mujer (de la serie el Silencio de Eros), 1965
Woman (of the Silence of Eros series)

Graphic Design:
Papersdoc

Printing and binding:
Grafos S.A.

ISBN: 978-1-940291-39-0

A CIP catalogue record for this book is available from the Library of Congress, Washington, DC, USA.

Acknowledgments:
Zilia Sánchez would like to thank Canal Street Studios and Casa Sofia de Puerto Rico, in particular, Meca Sorrentini, who has graciously allowed Zilia to use her space as a gallery and studio since 2009.
Galerie Lelong would like to thank Artists Space, New York, in particular Stefan Kalmár and Richard Birkett, César and Mima Reyes, Igor Da Costa, and the Museo de Arte Contemporáneo de Puerto Rico. The gallery would like to extend a warm thanks to Marimar Benítez for her support and scholarship.

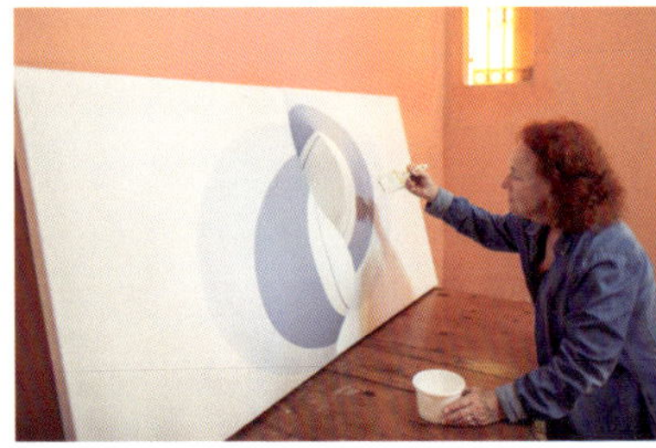